SAILING
DOWN THE
MOONBEAM

by

Mary Gottschalk

Rising Sun Press First Edition 2008

Cover Design by Sally Cooper Smith
Author Photo by James Fidler

Rising Sun Press
92 NE 64th Street
Des Moines, IA 50327
515-771-6675
www.risingsunpress.com

Manufactured in the United States of America

Second Printing

Library of Congress Control Number: 2008923027

ISBN: 978-0-9797997-2-3

To Tom,
without whom this story could never have happened

To Carol, Diane and Mary,
without whom this story would
never have been told

Acknowledgements

This is my story as I remember it, and all of the people and places I've described were part of that story. But some of the people may not want me to tell their story and for that reason I have changed the names of certain individuals—primarily the members of the Fearsome Foursome—and their boats. They, of course, will know who they are, and know that they made a most extraordinary time even better.

I acknowledge with gratitude the contributions of all the people who made this book possible. Without the unending support and occasional laughter of Carol Bodensteiner, Diane Glass, and Mary Nilsen, I would never have had the fortitude to finish this book. Others who read drafts and offered valuable critiques that made the book so much better include Bob Aukes, Pat Boddy, Susan Boe, Joanna Johnson, Mark Lunde, Sandi Parshall, Barbara Pearlman, Laura Sands and Mary Kay Shanley.

CONTENTS

Prologue   1

Part I   **Uncharted Waters**   5
Chapter 1   Anatomy of a Dream   7
Chapter 2   Cruising on the Rocks   17
Chapter 3   Choppy Waters   30
Chapter 4   Sailing on the Edge   40
Chapter 5   All Ahead Dead Slow   50

Part II   **Learning to Navigate**   59
Chapter 6   The Wind at our Back   61
Chapter 7   Setting the Stage   76
Chapter 8   On an Even Keel   86
Chapter 9   Sailing at the Edge—Again   108

Part III   **Fair Winds**   119
Chapter 10   The One That Got Away   121
Chapter 11   On a Lee Shore   129
Chapter 12   The Fearsome Foursome   138
Chapter 13   Paradise Found   147
Chapter 14   Paradise Revisited   163

Part IV   **Weathering the Storm**   169
Chapter 15   Shoal Waters   171
Chapter 16   Paradise Lost   184
Chapter 17   Adrift   192
Chapter 18   Charting a New Course   198

Itinerary   211

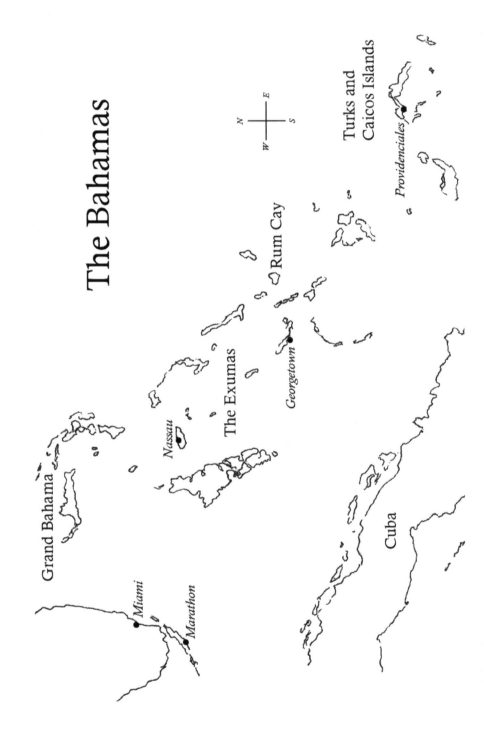

The Bahamas

Grand Bahama

Miami

Marathon

Nassau

The Exumas

Georgetown

Rum Cay

N
W · E
S

Cuba

Turks and
Caicos Islands

Providenciales

Panama Canal

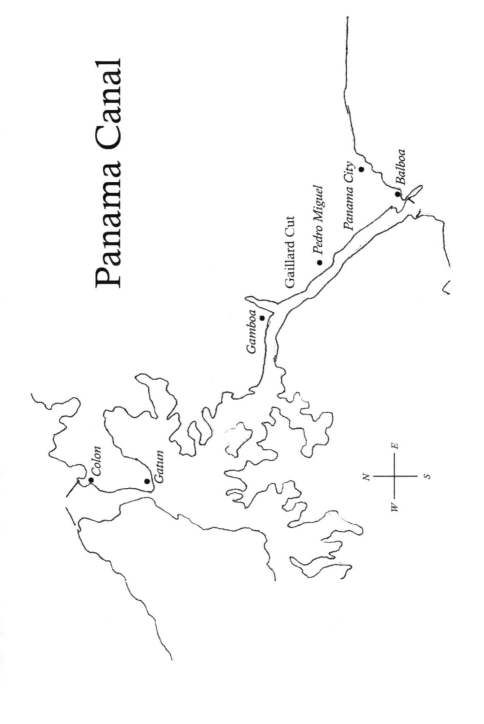

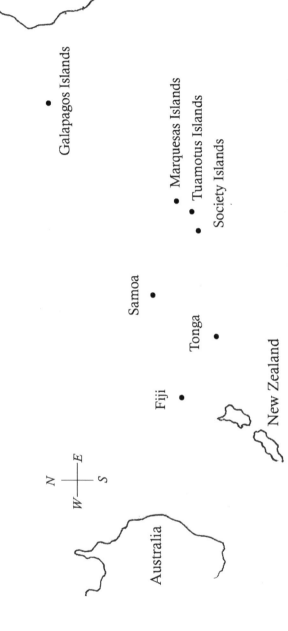

Pacific Ocean

South America

Galapagos Islands

Marquesas Islands
Tuamotus Islands
Society Islands

Samoa

Tonga

Fiji

New Zealand

Australia

N
W —— E
S

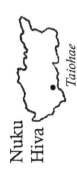

Nuku
Hiva

Taiohae

Ua
Pou

Ua
Huka

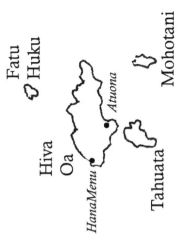

Fatu
Huku

Atuona

Hiva
Oa

HanaMenu

Mohotani

Tahuata

Fatu Hiva

N

E

W — S

Marquesas Islands

Bora Bora

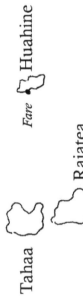
Tahaa

Raiatea

Fare Huahine

Tetiaroa

Moorea

Papeete

Tahiti

Maiao

Society Islands

N
W —|— E
S

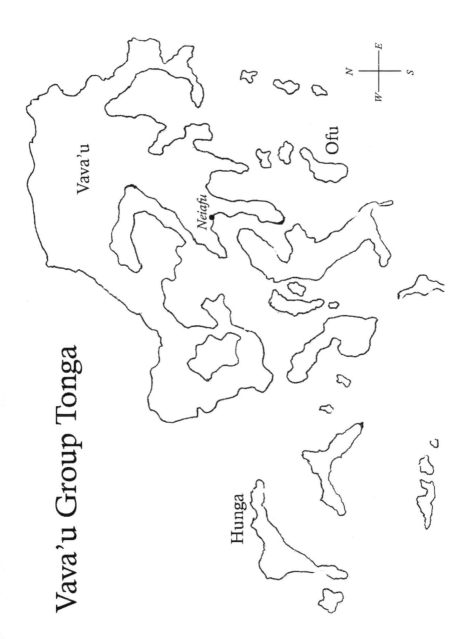

Vava'u Group Tonga

PROLOGUE

"HEY, Mary-pie, it's time to get up."
Tom's voice comes to me as if in a dream, somewhere very far away. "Go away, I don't have to go to work today," I mumble, hugging my pillow tighter.

"Com'on, no lollygagging. Get your bum out of this berth. You need to take the watch."

I open one eye to see Tom standing in the narrow aisle. "What time is it?" I ask.

"A bit after 3 a.m."

That wakes me up fast. I seldom sleep for more than five hours at a stretch. This is the third time since we'd left Bora Bora that Tom has to wake me after more than seven hours.

I roll out of the berth, clucking sympathetically, "You must be pooped. You've been on watch nearly eight hours. Did you doze at all?"

"Yeah, a bit in the last hour."

"Well, the berth's nice and warm, so crawl in," I say, slipping into a t-shirt and shorts without underwear.

As he closes his eyes, he says, "I left the stopwatch on the cabin top in the cockpit."

Like most couples cruising on the Pacific Ocean, we keep a four-hour daytime watch schedule, but we've worked out the night watch by trial-and-error. Generally, I go to sleep when I've finished dinner dishes, with Tom keeping watch until I wake up naturally around 1 a.m. I keep watch for the rest of the night and into the morning until he wakes up on his own, some days not until nearly lunchtime. On the rare occasion that I doze off, the alarm on the stopwatch wakes me every 19 minutes so I can scan the horizon to make sure we remain a safe distance from any ships.

I've come to love this routine, eight to 10 hours of solitude, at one with the sea and the sky, my private time with both the night and the day. The nights are magical, increasingly so as we move southward. Each night, coming up on deck, that first glimpse of the Milky Way takes my breath away, surprising me anew with its density and brightness, a glittering white stripe painted across the star-studded sky. As I watch the satellites drifting ever-so-slowly between and through the constellations, I often find myself in a mystical space, a cosmic place of absolute silence and serenity from which I peer down on the tiny speck that is *Salieri* making her way across the vast ocean.

Many nights I actively study the stars, matching what I see through my binoculars with the textbook descriptions of the constellations in the southern sky. The night sky is my neighborhood, and I've come to know it as I knew the street I lived on as a child. I never tire of exploring the dark patch, the size of a small plum from where I sit, near the edge of the Magellanic Cloud. Astronomers believe it's a "black hole" that sucks in everything that comes into its orbit. Every night, I check to see if any stars have appeared in it. None so far.

I am surprised one night in early March to find a large, whirling mass in the sky, a nebula I'd never seen before. It isn't in any of our reference books. I watch it night after night, wondering what it is and why it has so suddenly appeared. Only when we arrive in Tahiti do I learn the answer—it's a supernova that has just arrived in our solar system, the now-visible remnants of a cosmic explosion 170,000 light years away.

Best of all is the moon, its reflection a shimmering white-gold path in the water ahead of our bow as we sail in a southwesterly direction. I know, of course, that the moon isn't always out, that the arc it traces across the sky puts it behind us for part of the night even when it is up. But in my mind's eye, being on watch at night means sailing down that ribbon of light dancing in the water, imagining all the magical places that lay at the end of the moonbeam.

Nearly as appealing is the gradually brightening sky at dawn, the web of multicolored highlights spreading slowly from east to west across the rippled surface of the sea. It's the time of day when the dolphins come to call, sometimes only two or three of them, sometimes a school of a dozen or more. Their high-pitched squeaks have a conversational rhythm. From the many times they've led us through the passes in coral reefs, I'm sure they know what they are trying to say.

My suspicions are confirmed one spectacular morning when arrival of the dolphins paints the sea white as far as I can see on either side of *Salieri*. For nearly half an hour, hundreds of dolphins entertain me with their swoops and dives and calls. And then, in the time it takes to blink, they're gone, the surface of water unbroken. As I nurse my disappointment, six dolphins all in a row burst through the surface about 10 yards away. They do a tail walk worthy of the Rockettes. They are waving good-bye.

Oddly, the sunrise itself almost always disappoints me. All-too-brief and predictable, a small compact orb glows gold for less than a minute before it breaks above the horizon. Rarely do I see the swirling reds and pinks that I associate with the dawn of a new day. But those colors belong to a world of changing weather, of variable humidity, of dust and air pollution. On the Pacific in July, the weather never changes and there is little to pollute the air. Although I miss the dramatic sunrises, it's a trade-off I'm happy to make.

As I fix myself a cup of tea and some sweet biscuits, I hear Tom snoring. His eight hours on watch, much too long to be alone at night, bespeaks a kind of caring new in our 15-year-long relationship. With my cup of tea in hand, I walk forward to the cabin. As I watch him sleep, I think my heart will burst with love.

Eventually, I go back up on deck. With dawn still more than an hour away, I can see only a tiny sliver of grey on the horizon. As I watch the dawn creep into the sky, it strikes me that many things besides my sleeping patterns have changed. As our cruise has taken us farther and farther from the world I grew up in, I've tossed overboard one after another of my childhood fears, one after another of the unproductive habits I used to deal with those fears. I've stopped expecting Tom to fill all my needs. I can hardly remember what life was like when I defined myself in terms of a Wall Street career. I rarely think about my mother, and her approval—or the lack of it—no longer dominates my life. I have no desire for something better to come along. What I have is just fine.

It has taken me 40 years to reach this place of contentment. Will it last another 40 years?

PART I

UNCHARTED WATERS

CHAPTER 1

ANATOMY OF A DREAM

EXPERIENCED sailors don't expect a major problem on the fourth day of a five-year sailing voyage. We certainly didn't.

It happened just after lunch at Schaffer's Canal House, a landmark café in the middle of the Chesapeake and Delaware Canal. As I backed *Salieri* away from the dock, I checked to make sure we'd clear the boat behind us. I turned the wheel hard to the left. No response. I spun it hard to the right. Nothing.

My temples throbbing, I shouted to Tom, on the foredeck coiling dock lines. "Tom, we're drifting downstream on the current." By the time I finished my sentence, Tom had tossed a line to a passerby on the dock and manually hauled our 37-foot sailboat back to shore.

I paced the deck while Tom went below to check the engine and the steering gear. When he reappeared in his swim trunks, his snorkel mask perched on his head, he said cheerily, "Well, Mary-pie, everything looks fine below. So, I need to check the propeller."

"Yuck," I said, wrinkling my nose, "you're really going into that oily green muck we're floating in?"

Tom shrugged. "No other way to check the prop."

The throbbing in my temples grew louder as he disappeared below the surface. When he finally reappeared a minute later, he asked for the iron mallet. "The propeller shaft has backed out of its coupling to the engine. I have to hammer it back in place."

Using a long line, I tied the heavy mallet to a deck cleat, then handed it down. Tom disappeared again. As I listened anxiously to the muffled sound of metal clanking against metal six feet underwater, I congratulated myself on picking a husband who loved a challenge. Twice, he came up for air. The third time, he shouted out, "Mission accomplished."

After he'd had a long, hot shower, we headed once again for the Chesapeake Bay. While I steered, he lolled in the cockpit, nursing a cold Anchor Steam beer, his faded orange-and-yellow sailing hat propped on his forehead to block the sun. "How'd you know what to do," I asked from the helm, "when you couldn't see more than an inch away?"

"Hey, I've been pulling stuff apart and putting it back together since I was five. After a while, you just know how things are supposed to look." He gave me a boyish grin. "Or…in this case, feel." After a long, slow swig on his beer, he continued solemnly, "I'd be happier if I knew why it happened."

My shoulder muscles twitched. "You mean it could it happen again?"

He closed his eyes. "Yeah, it could."

Our trip was the culmination of a dream Tom and I had shared for years. But the timing of our trip, like so many milestones in our life together, resulted from a spur-of-the-moment decision, this one made on a brutally cold Sunday night in late January 1985.

Tom had the wheel of our blue Fiat sports car as we drove back to suburban New York City from our weekend house in the Berkshires. The trip, a bit over two hours, took us through one after another of the storybook colonial villages in the Hudson River valley. That night, we'd talked mostly about money, a tedious but necessary task.

Despite our dual careers in finance, neither of us had any noticeable talent in the stock market. So when Tom had left his job in venture capital two years earlier, he'd kept his investment in the firm's partnership. We planned to use the money to buy a sailboat and sail around the world when the partnership terminated in 1995. Now, to our dismay, the firm had decided to cash him out, 10 years early, leaving the money sitting idle in a bank. After two hours, we'd failed to come up with a single sexy idea for what to do with it.

I hated talking about money. We should, I thought, just buy the damn boat and go sailing now.

Startled, I realized I'd spoken my thought aloud. I looked over at Tom to see if he'd heard me. A small hollow had formed in his right cheek, a sure sign of his concentration. As we pulled onto our exit ramp, he grinned. "You know, Mary-pie, that's exactly what we should do. Do you s'pose we could be ready to leave by the fall, before the weather turns?"

Without missing a beat, I replied, "We'd have to work like dogs for the next six or seven months, but I bet we could get out of here in September."

Spur-of-the-moment decisions came naturally to us. One of the first took place on a Saturday in October 1972, nine months after Tom and I met on a ski slope in Vermont. Stretched out on the striped velvet couch in my studio apartment on the Upper West Side, his feet propped on the old green steamer trunk I used as a coffee table, he was absorbed in the morning paper. From behind the wall of newsprint, I heard his disembodied voice.

"Mary, there's an ad for a two-bedroom apartment on 72nd Street, just off Central Park. We could walk to work through the park. Let's check it out this afternoon."

At the glass-topped table in the bay window, sipping my coffee and trying to lean into the small patch of morning sun that eked its way between the apartment buildings, I replied with curiosity. "I thought you liked living in Murray Hill."

The voice again. "I do. But trudging back and forth between Murray Hill and the Upper West Side is getting old. I feel like a nomad."

I shivered, thrilled he'd move to the West Side to be near me. "But why go from a studio to a two-bedroom apartment? Did you get a raise I don't know about?"

From behind the paper, he said, "Don't you want a spare room for guests or a study?"

My cup hit the table rather harder than I intended, coffee sloshing out. "Are you talking about an apartment for you ...," my heart was banging against the walls of my chest, "...or for us?"

He lowered the paper and peered over top of his tortoise-shell glasses with a look that said the answer should have been obvious. "For us, of course...why would I need a two-bedroom apartment by myself?"

I shivered again. I often thought I'd fallen in love with Tom, a man who smiled with his eyes as well as his mouth, the first time I saw him at the next table in the ski resort cafeteria. We exchanged glances several times during lunch, but our first conversation came when we shared a ski lift in the afternoon.

That day, a Monday, was a bank holiday, so it did not surprise me to find he also worked for Citibank and knew of me, at least by name. As we rode up the steep slope, we compared notes on the Sunday *New York Times* crossword puzzle. I was impressed that he'd already finished it. When we discovered that neither of us had seen *Deep Throat*, months after its release, a movie date seemed obvious.

We had a lot in common. Tom, an avid reader, was logical, analytical and naturally curious. Conservative with money, he wanted to get value for what he spent. Our resonance was greatest, however, in being firstborns, overachievers who'd come to New York City determined to succeed in the world of high finance. His father, a man I soon found to be sour and mean-spirited, had raised Tom to measure success by how much money he made, how big a raise he got, what percentage his bonus was. My mother, for whom nothing I ever did was good enough, had instilled in me a desperate need to please. We both worked long hours, determined to do the right thing in the right way, worried constantly about being found wanting.

But it was our differences that bound me to him. He never met anyone he couldn't talk to about something—wine, history, sports, sailing, physics, whatever—and his easy way with people paved the way for me, an introvert invariably ill at ease with strangers. Even at age 40, ten years married and professionally successful, casual conversation with strangers still seemed all but impossible. I remained a prisoner of a pervasive anxiety, the legacy of a mother who found my ideas stupid, of schoolmates who mocked me for being so smart.

Tom complemented me in other ways as well. His instinctive view of every problem as an opportunity took the edge off my frustration when things didn't go according to plan—he could find a way to have fun changing a flat tire in a rainstorm. I saw his implacable good humor as a powerful antidote to my tendency toward depression.

That Saturday morning in October, I couldn't imagine life

without his boyish sense of possibility, his omnipresent good humor. I loved his morning smile, his mop of curly, caramel-colored hair, and the hollow space on the sides of his tight, high butt. But I wasn't sure he loved me. We'd never talked about it. Even so, I went to see the apartment and signed a lease that afternoon. Two weeks later, I merged my life into his.

By the time we parked the car that cold January night, I was having second thoughts about upending our lives. Waves of them. Being the Chief Financial Officer for a commodities importer made me successful in an era when professional women were a rarity. If I dropped out at age 40, could I ever get back in? I had no desire to be a waitress for the rest of my life.

Coming up the stairs, my concerns stretched beyond work. I loved my weekly tennis matches with Barbara. I loved the opera and the ballet, and now, after 10 years, I'd finally graduated to good subscription seats. And the Berkshire farmhouse, nearly perfect after a decade of restoration done mostly with our sweat equity. And my garden, the sight of the first daffodils in the spring, the feel of the rich, loamy soil on my hands.

And then, of course, there was Tom. He liked military history and horror movies. I liked biography and art films. He was athletic and competitive while I exercised only as much as necessary to keep fit. Sailing was one of the few activities we did together, but even that served us in different ways. I loved the timelessness of life on the water, as well as the opportunity to see out-of-the-way places. Tom was far more interested in getting the best from a powerful piece of machinery. We sailed in the same space, at the same time, heading in the same direction, but we were rarely taking the same trip. Could we manage to hold each other's interest if we spent 24 hours a day together?

The literature on long-term cruising was not encouraging.

Living on a boat creates a hothouse environment that can kill an otherwise healthy relationship. One problem is the lack of privacy, the obligation to consider the other person's needs all day every day. Another is the pressure to be all things to your companion, all the time, simply because no one else is around to provide relief.

The clunk of Tom's key in the lock of our apartment door brought me back to Bronxville. "Were you really serious about going sailing?" I asked. "Can you walk away from your consulting business...your wine cellar...your Jaguar?"

"You bet." he said without hesitation. "Are you having second thoughts?"

"I dunno. It's a pretty outrageous thing to do at our age."

Resting his hands on my shoulders, his eyes searched mine. "Mary, we've talked for years about going cruising. This money allows us to do it while we're still young and healthy. A door's just opened for us. If we're afraid to walk through it now, we probably won't have the guts to do it when we're older."

I cocked my head, returning his gaze. "So..." I peeled the words out one by one, "I...guess...we're...going...sailing." My gut twisted tighter with every word. I had a lot more to lose than when I signed that apartment lease 12 years earlier.

Waiting for sleep that night, I recalled our conversation after seeing the film *Amadeus*. In an early scene, Salieri, an old man in a wheelchair, reminisces about Mozart. With some bitterness, he observes that "the curse of my life has been to recognize genius in someone else—and to know I didn't have it."

He's talking about me, I'd thought. Despite my successes, I knew I'd never be mover-and-shaker material. In the dark theater, I turned to see Tom wink at me.

On the way home, Tom asked, "Did Salieri strike as much of a chord with you as he did with me?"

"Yup," I replied. "We've done well for ourselves. But neither of us will make it to the top in this town."

He nodded, reluctant to say what we both knew—that each

13

of us, in our own way, was limited by personality as much as by brains or ability. I had no talent for social chitchat, too impatient to thread my way through the politics of major success. Tom's social skills masked an insensitivity to how people felt and what motivated them. And in New York, the rule was up or out. Every job represented a rung on the ladder to somewhere. If you didn't want to keep climbing, you had to move out of the way so someone headed for the top could use that rung for awhile.

Tom nodded. "You know, when we finally do go sailing, let's name our yacht *Salieri.*"

As I drifted off to sleep, I thought that leaving New York in September might be exactly the right thing to do.

The next week was typical of my life in New York. I worked 10–12 hours each day, after getting up at 5 a.m. to do a half-mile swim. My job, working for an often irascible commodity trader, left me exhausted. By the time I got home and had dinner, I could do little more than fall into bed. Several times that week, I dreamt of being on a treadmill, running hard to stay in place. Even as the recurrent dream urged me to go sailing, I wondered whether I could survive without the intellectual stimulation of a job, without a professional purpose?

I hardly saw Tom. He had an overnight business trip early in the week and played squash after work two of the remaining evenings. His one evening home, he worked on our taxes. Our first chance to discuss the logistics of a long-term cruise came en route to the Berkshires the following Friday night.

The to-do list was daunting…find and buy a boat…equip it for ocean cruising…stock it with spare parts, medical supplies and books…assemble an itinerary and order navigational charts…plan menus and buy provisions. Then, too, we'd have to unravel the fabric of more than a decade in New York. The final bits of the renovation on the Berkshire house had to be completed. We'd need a long-term tenant as well as a property manager. The Bronxville apartment would have to be sold.

Furniture, rugs, clothes and financial records would have to go into storage. We'd have to arrange to have mail collected, bills paid and taxes filed for the next five years.

"Can we possibly get it all done by September, especially if we both continue to work?"

Tom seemed unfazed. "We'll be fine," he insisted, "if I can find a boat by the spring."

My ambivalence continued throughout that weekend. During a brunch with neighbors on Saturday, I realized once again how much I depended on my friends to share my highs and support me in the lows. Over the years, I had learned that the price I paid for Tom's consistent good humor was his lack of interest in my emotional ups and downs. How well would I cope if Tom was my only emotional support system?

My doubts mounted as I sat through a Japanese film at the Art Museum in Pittsfield on Friday night. Could life on a sailboat possibly offer enough variety to keep me interested? But then on Saturday afternoon, while I sanded and painted the window seat I'd built under the bay in the living room, I decided sailing was the right thing to do. Gazing out over the snow-covered stream, I realized we'd never, in a decade, found time to fish it for trout. As I finished the molding around the window, I heard Tom drive into the garage. Not once during the previous summer had we found time to indulge in the sheer pleasure of driving his Jaguar, a gorgeous and powerful car, along the serpentine mountain roads. If we went sailing, I would finally have the time to enjoy the beauty around me.

In late March, we found *Salieri* in a Staten Island marina, her natural teak decks and bright red sail covers blanketed by six inches of snow. Below decks, we found a warm, spacious saloon with a gleaming copper and Delft teapot bubbling on the stove.

The bulkheads, richly oiled teak, were lined with yards of bookshelves. The galley had double sinks, a four-burner stove and an oven large enough to cook a turkey. Everywhere I looked, I found a drawer with an elegant teak pull or a cupboard with a teak-and-rattan door. Under every seat or berth I discovered cavernous lockers. Love at first sight!

We left on September 7th, a crisp fall Saturday in 1985, with friends from more than a decade mingling on the dock at the Larchmont Yacht Club, a bit north of the city. When we could not delay any longer, I spun the chrome knob to unlock the steering wheel. With a flourish, Tom, wearing the faded orange-and-yellow checked sailing hat he'd acquired in his teens, released the dock lines that bound us to the only world we'd known as a couple. As we pulled away, I heard a champagne bottle break against our bow.

I remember very little of that day once we left Larchmont. To get to the Atlantic, we had to sail down the East River, past the magnificent Manhattan skyline, past the landmarks of our courtship and marriage. I was oblivious to its beauty and symbolism.

What I do remember is the United Airlines jet, disconcertingly low in the sky, on the glide path for LaGuardia Airport. I wondered whether its wheels would snag our 62-foot mast. I must have been holding my breath, because I felt a physical sense of relief, a sudden easing of the pressure in my lungs, when the plane had made its way across the river. In retrospect, I realize that the scene captured both extremes of our life…the plane heading for the center of our cultural universe, our small sailboat leaving it behind.

CHAPTER 2

CRUISING ON
THE ROCKS

TOM'S prediction about the propeller came all too true. Three days after the first prop problem, we headed into an Annapolis marina late on a sunny Saturday afternoon, with boats bumper to bumper. As we reversed the engine to slow our turn into our assigned slip, we lost steerageway and drifted into a glossy blue and white cabin cruiser. Within moments, several small power boats appeared and maneuvered the once-again-powerless *Salieri* into a slip.

With boat traffic dead slow, we did no damage to the cruiser or to *Salieri*. But good sailors don't drift into other boats. I wanted to disappear into the ether.

"Why's the prop backing out?" I wailed as I picked at my dinner, pushing wads of pasta around on the plate. "It worked fine in New York."

"I think it's a problem with reverse gear," he suggested. "We'll just stop using it until we get to Charleston."

"Don't we need reverse to set the hook when we anchor?" I queried more than a little disingenuously, knowing perfectly well that we did.

Tom shrugged. "Yeah. But it'd cost a fortune to get it fixed here in Annapolis. We'll just be careful between here and Charleston."

The next morning, Tom dove into the water and hammered the prop back into place once again. As we headed out, he patted my hand. "Don't worry, kiddo. We'll be fine."

I wanted to believe him. After all, Tom had been sailing on big boats, on big bodies of water for 15 years before we met. Of course he knew what needed to be done. A mere eight days into our five-year dream, I tried to convince myself, not altogether successfully, that I had nothing to worry about.

A week of sunny days and calm anchorages in the lower Chesapeake Bay allayed much of my anxiety. Between gorging on fresh fish and crab, we scoured local bookstores for history and fiction about colonial times on the East Coast. Over meals, we took turns reading aloud, sharing tales of scoundrels who lured unwitting ships onto the shoals off the Outer Banks at night by walking mules along the sandy beaches, their saddlebags hung with lighted candles or lanterns to replicate a mooring light.

Approaching the Intracoastal Waterway just south of Norfolk, we assumed we'd left our troubles behind us. The Waterway—in sailors' parlance, the ICW or the "ditch"— passes through some of the most spectacular waterfront scenery in the U.S. Relying on a series of man-made canals to link the rivers and bays along the East Coast, the ICW allows private boats and commercial barges to travel between New Jersey and Florida with minimal exposure to Atlantic storms. With dozens of as-yet-unopened boxes of marine equipment, provisions and spare parts piled haphazardly on every berth, we couldn't risk bad weather on the open ocean. The ICW, by far the safer choice, would make our trip considerably longer than the ocean route. Four hundred miles under engine power on a sailboat didn't sound like fun.

Now, leaving the Chesapeake for the 12-day canal trip from Norfolk to Charleston, I was perched on the cabin top, my elbow wedged against the boom to steady the binoculars. "Gees, there's a million buoys out there," I moaned. "I haven't a clue which ones mark the canal entrance." With considerable hesitation, I said, "It's got to be south of us. Let's go that way and see if it gets any more obvious."

Tom adjusted the wheel. "South it is. I'll take it dead slow, just in case."

Ten minutes later, I spied the ICW markers. "Tom, we're heading for Willoughby Bay. The ICW is off our bow at about two o'clock."

"You got it." He spun the wheel a quarter turn.

Less than a minute later, we glided to a halt, our six-foot keel ignominiously aground in five and a half feet of water. We may have been experienced sailors, but neither of us had remembered to check the chart, which clearly indicated the shallow patch between the two channels.

In an effort to get *Salieri* back afloat without using reverse gear, we swung the solid maple boom all the way out to port, hoping the weight would heel us over enough to float. *Salieri* shuddered as the keel pushed up through the soft mud. Still aground. As a last desperate measure, Tom crawled out to the end of the 16-foot boom. His extra 170 pounds did the trick! I gunned the engine. Off we went, without damage and without using reverse gear.

That scene set the stage for life in the ICW, every bit as tedious as we expected. The edges of the six-foot deep canal tended to silt up and were littered with fallen trees and submerged limbs. Our six-foot keel gave us no margin for error. Two or three times a day, *Salieri* jolted to a stop, her keel caught on the bottom, and then lurched forward again.

Mid-afternoon on the second day, a heavily laden coal

barge came toward us from the south. To pass, we had to move well to the west side of the shallow waterway. I held my breath as the barge, several hundred feet long, slid slowly by. About to start breathing again, I realized I'd been staring at the same drooping branch on a willow tree for perhaps 10 seconds. "Tom," I moaned, "we're aground again."

Undaunted, he said, "Help me get the spare anchor into the dinghy. I'll row it out into the center of the canal, ahead of us. We'll pull ourselves up on it, back into deep water." Half an hour later, we were underway again.

Two days later, we breathed a collective sigh of relief as we exited the canal into Albemarle Sound, just south of the Virginia–North Carolina border. We shook out the sails and let *Salieri* run free. I luxuriated in the feel of the wind on my skin, sometimes a gentle zephyr that barely ruffled the fine hairs on my arm, other times a gust so strong I had to brace myself against it. I listened for the sound of the water along the hull, rushing noisily when the boat picked up speed, gurgling softly when our pace slowed. I felt the temperature fluctuate from warm to cool and back again, as the changing angle of our heel moved me between sunlight and the shadow of the mainsail. The muscles in my back and legs flexed constantly, responding to even the smallest motion of the boat.

My delight proved to be short-lived. As we approached the south end of the Sound, I checked the weather. Horrified, I scrambled up to the deck. "Tom, Hurricane Gloria is supposed to hit the Outer Banks tomorrow afternoon. That's only 70 miles away. We're heading right for it. Should we go back north?"

Tom, his back against the cockpit wall, sat steering with his bare feet. He shook his head vigorously. "No way I'm going back there." Reaching for the chart, he pointed to the Alligator River at the south end of the Sound. "The Alligator has lots of small creeks flowing into it. We'll go up one of them until we run out of water. We can't avoid the wind, but at least we won't have any waves."

Our chosen creek, its banks lined with a dense cypress forest that would shelter us from the wind, wound back on itself several times. We inched our way up to the headwaters and anchored in seven feet of water, much too shallow for waves to develop no matter how strong the wind. According to the chart, the bottom was pure mud. A perfect hurricane hole!

And a gorgeous spot besides! The water sparkled, at once crystal clear and midnight black, its color drawn from the ebony sap of the lush and stately cypress trees surrounding our little cove. As darkness fell, we fixed pork chops and fresh salad and opened a bottle of wine. The gentle breeze and bright moon in an indigo, star-studded sky made it hard to believe a catastrophic storm waited in the wings.

Gray, rainy weather the next morning made it easier to believe, but the wind remained light. According to the updates from the National Weather Service, the storm was intensifying, but traveling northward more slowly than expected. By noon, landfall had been pushed back to late evening.

The day dragged on. I tried to read, but couldn't make sense of the words. After struggling through a few pages, I gave up and began to unpack boxes of provisions and organize the food lockers. Tom unpacked and stowed boxes of tools. He checked and rechecked the hatches, the sails and the lashing on the jugs of water and fuel on deck, and then checked them yet again. Twice, we rowed to shore and trudged through the dense forest despite the rain and mud, desperate for something to occupy us while we waited.

Mid-afternoon, Tom rowed the dinghy out to check the anchor for the fourth time. A few moments later, he called out, "Mary, I want to put out a second anchor at a 45 degree angle to the first. Help me get it into the dinghy."

As I fed the spare anchor with 100 feet of line into the dinghy, I tried to visualize how the two anchors would work.

"Won't the anchor lines cross if the wind direction changes?"
I asked.

"No," he said perfunctorily. "The anchors will pivot as we
swing. Don't worry. We'll be fine." I couldn't quite picture it,
and made a mental note to have Tom diagram it for me. To my
regret, by the time he'd climbed back on board, I'd forgotten.

It was almost a relief, as we fixed dinner, to hear that the
storm had reached Morehead City, 120 miles to the south. We
did dishes, checked the hatches and portholes one more time,
and settled in the cockpit to watch the storm approach. From
time to time, we commented on the wind or the absence of
wind, the rain or the absence of rain, the steadily darkening
sky. We had no energy for serious conversation and occasionally one or the other of us dozed off. Mostly, we fretted.

Around midnight, the wind picked up. We listened with
fascination as the Weather Service described the scene in
Buxton, 40 miles away, where the vacuum at the leading edge
of the hurricane had sucked the water, all 30 feet of it, out
of the harbor, leaving dozens of fishing boats careened on the
muddy bottom. At 2 a.m., the full force of the storm hit us.
Our wind gauge read 70 mph, the wind stripping the surface of
the cove, flinging microscopic arrows of water sharp enough to
draw blood when they hit bare skin. We had to go below. We
liked being warm and dry but found it far more unnerving than
being on deck. We could feel every shudder as *Salieri* strained
on her anchor, hear every rattle as she pitched back and forth
erratically.

About 4 a.m., an eerie silence drew us back up on deck
where we found a starry sky—the eye of the storm directly
overhead. Ten minutes later, the wind and rain hit us at full
force from the opposite direction. We went below again.

Tom lay down on the settee with a book, but sat up almost
immediately. "Mary, does our motion feel odd?"

I stood still, letting my body sway with *Salieri's* movement.
"Yeah...we're rolling. I bet the anchors aren't holding."

Grabbing his wet gear, Tom raced up to the cockpit. From my dry spot in the companionway, I switched on the deck lights. With rain pouring off his hood, Tom put the engine in low gear and pointed *Salieri's* bow into the wind, a move designed to take pressure off the anchor. The rolling motion stopped. I raised my hand to give him a victory sign when I heard a heavy metallic clank.

"What was that?" I shouted over the noise of the engine and the wind. The muscles in my shoulders locked as we started to roll again.

No answer. I watched Tom play with the speed control for a few moments, but he had no effect on our motion. Slamming his left hand against the steering wheel, he cut the engine. "Damn it to hell. The prop's backed out again."

Stripping off his dripping wet gear, he muttered, "...nothing we can do without an engine. I'm going to bed," he said, his shoulders slumped. I'd never seen him look so dejected.

Too jittery to sleep, I stretched out on the settee, listening to the shrieking wind, trying to breathe as deeply as I could. After about 20 minutes, the rolling motion stopped. I assumed we'd been blown aground, but I could see nothing when I peered out the porthole into the rain-swept blackness. Feeling as discouraged as Tom had looked, I took two aspirin and crawled in next to him. He turned wordlessly and stretched his arm over my shoulder. A little before dawn, the wind eased and I fell asleep.

About 10 a.m., I woke to bright sun, clear skies and the sound of Tom on the foredeck above me. Opening the hatch, I peered out. Close enough to touch, I saw two magnificent cypress trees, their thick green branches draped over the deck, our bow firmly wedged between their trunks.

When he heard the hatch open, Tom turned and gave me an impresario's bow from the waist, brandishing his right arm toward the trees. "How do you like the décor? It's a one-day-only hurricane special, perfect for drying wet gear."

I laughed out loud. After only a few hours sleep, the imperturbable Tom had returned.

While Tom fixed English muffins and cantaloupe, I radioed a salvage service and hung our wet clothes on the trees to dry. After breakfast, he retrieved the anchors, which no longer served any purpose. When he hauled the first anchor up, the line was tangled with the line from the second anchor. As he pulled the snarled lines into the dinghy, he drifted steadily closer to the stern, the site of the loud clank the night before. Peering into the black water, he fumed, "Dammit to hell."

"What's the matter?" I asked, already knowing the answer.

"One of the anchor lines wrapped around the prop shaft when I powered forward in the dark last night." Stripping off his shirt and jeans, Tom said, "I'll dive in and see if I can untangle it. If that doesn't work, we'll have to cut it."

While Tom freed the anchor line, I sat in the cockpit with a pencil and paper, determined to figure out the motion of *Salieri's* swing with the two anchors. I soon realized that when the eye passed over us, the wind had come back with such force that *Salieri* had swung 180 degrees in only a few seconds, far too quickly for the anchors to pivot. When they broke loose, one of the anchor lines must have been drifting under our hull. It would have caught in the prop when Tom put the engine on.

I remembered my question the day before. Then, as so many times during years of sailing vacations, I'd simply relied on Tom's experience. Now, in the shade of the cypress trees, I knew I needed to ask if I didn't understand.

By the time the salvage boat arrived, Tom had the lines untangled, the prop pounded back in and the anchors stowed. It took several hours to free us, using two 500 HP engines to literally blow away the four feet of mud that encased our hull and held us fast against the trees. Once afloat, we breathed a short-lived sigh of relief when the engine turned over without delay. As soon as we put the engine in gear, we heard a loud, irregular thunk-thunk-thunk from the vicinity of the propeller.

With the salvage boat behind us in case the engine gave out, we limped slowly to Belhaven, N.C., where we hauled *Salieri* out on an old-fashioned marine railway. The hull was undamaged but the propeller shaft sported a visible bend. Repairs would take at least three days, maybe more.

There wasn't much to do or see in Belhaven, a tiny southern town whose sole claim to fame seemed to be its abundant supplies of fresh crab and lobster available at ridiculously low prices. While we waited for the repairs, we continued to unpack boxes and organize stowage and socialized with the other denizens of the marina, who offered us heaps of advice on the cruising life. Two bits of advice stand out.

One came from Alan, the harbormaster, who was reviewing our detailed itinerary as we dug into a lunchtime platter of fresh crabs. Glancing first at Tom, then at me, he said, "You guys are way too organized. Nothing in a cruiser's life ever works out the way you planned. You'll drive yourself nuts if you try to stick to this tight a schedule."

Waving a forkful of crabmeat in the air, he continued. "Besides, the best experiences will be the ones you didn't plan for. If you decide everything in advance, you'll miss the best part of the journey."

I felt a rush of adrenaline. It sounded like he had just trashed the itinerary we'd spent so many hours laying out, one that would allow us to see what we wanted to see in the time available. But I couldn't dismiss his advice, since two weeks into our dream cruise, we had already fallen a week behind. Waiting in Belhaven, we had no idea how valuable his advice would prove to be.

The other nugget of wisdom came from Ingrid, half of a husband-and-wife team that sailed to the U.S. from Germany. Walking back to *Salieri* from the marina office, I saw her sitting in the cockpit of *Westphalia* and waved.

"Why are you walking so fast?" she asked. "Is something wrong?"

"No, I always walk fast," I replied. "New Yorkers do that."

With a mock grimace, she said. "But this isn't New York." Winking, she continued, "The point of cruising is to see the world. You should try walking slow enough to see as it goes by."

I could feel my ears reddening, a mix of anger and embarrassment. But in the days that followed, I replayed her words. Walking fast and talking fast worked in the frenetic arena of New York, but served no purpose here. It had taken a stranger to point out that my New York persona might hinder my ability to enjoy this adventure. For months after leaving Belhaven, I consciously practiced speaking more slowly, lowering the decibel of my voice, sauntering rather than striding. Twenty years later, I still walk slower and talk more softly than I did that day.

When we finally headed back into the ICW on October 3rd, with an almost new propeller shaft and a good-as-new reverse gear, I was in high spirits, assuming we'd used up our lifetime quota of bad luck. I took the next grounding, again alongside a passing barge, in stride.

And then came Beaufort.

I had the wheel, aiming down the middle of the harbor channel when we jolted to a stop. Tom bolted up from the saloon where he'd been cataloguing spare parts. "What the hell did you do?"

I felt like I'd been slapped. In our 13 years together, he'd never spoken to me like that. "I didn't *do* anything. We're aground in the center of the channel."

"Goddammit, Mary," he barked out, "you don't go aground in the middle of a seven-foot deep marked channel."

"Well, sometimes you do," I retorted, annoyed at his lack

of faith in my steering ability, but still worried that I might accidentally have drifted out of the channel.

To prove his point, Tom took bearings on nearby landmarks. In fact, the bearings confirmed we were in mid-channel, exactly where we were supposed to be. "Apparently," he informed me without apology, "the channel has silted up."

His behavior, however infuriating, was so atypical of my normally good-humored companion, I stifled my indignation.

An hour later, after winching *Salieri* through nearly 100 yards of the silted-in channel, we approached the town dock, where we had to turn left into our assigned slip. With a 15-knot crosswind, we'd need a lot of engine power to make the turn without the bow blowing off to the right. But with too much power, we'd crash into the dock.

Tom took the helm. My palms were sweaty as I positioned myself on the bow with a dock line. As we made the turn, *Salieri's* bow slid steadily to the right. I didn't have a hope in hell of reaching the dock with my line. I heard Tom shout, "Goddammit, Mary, can't you do anything right?"

I had no time to be shocked by his words or his tone. *Salieri's* bow had already nosed into the adjacent slip. With every bit of strength I could muster, I heaved the end of the line to a teenager fishing on the dock. With his help, we got *Salieri* lined up in her own slip. Onlookers must have thought we were the three stooges less one.

Once we got *Salieri* squared away, we headed into town to get some exercise, but I have no memory of where we walked or what we saw. I could focus on nothing but the mess we'd made of trying to dock. In nearly a decade of sailing together, we had not had as many mishaps as we'd suffered in our first three weeks. Something was wrong, but I didn't know what.

Over dinner, I asked in a conciliatory tone, "Tom, is something bothering you? Why were you so angry at me today?"

Tom sounded self-righteous. "Mary, I'm tired of your not

holding up your end of this boat. I needed you to get a line on that piling."

"I couldn't reach the piling from the bow." I chose not to point out that he hadn't put on enough power.

Tom shot back, "Why didn't you throw a lariat around it?"

I responded defensively. "I've never been able to throw a lariat. You know that. I'm sorry I can't do all the things you can on a boat."

"You certainly can't," he shot back.

The crosswinds, along with my hurt feelings, were still with us the next morning. "Tom," I pleaded, "Let's walk through what will happen when we leave."

Tom dismissed my request with a wave of his hand. "Just do what I tell you." Handing me the line holding our bow to the dock, he said in a peremptory tone, "Hold this until I tell you to let go."

"What if the bow swings to the right again as we back away?" I asked, feeling the tension on the line from the wind pushing the bow toward the adjacent slip.

"Dammit, the bow will be fine if you keep the line taut."

Tom backed us slowly out of the slip. When we'd gone about halfway back, Tom called out, "Okay, let 'er go! I did. The bow promptly swung to the right, toward the middle piling.

I heard Tom scream, "Fend off the bow. **MARY, FEND OFF!"**

I moved toward the piling, but with 23,000 pounds of fiberglass and wood behind our swing, I couldn't possibly hold us off with my bare hands. I watched helplessly as the bow hit the piling, crunching the aluminum rail inward.

Tom yelled again. "Dammit, why didn't you fend us off?"

Trembling with both shock and fury, I shouted back. "Don't yell at me! I asked you to do a dry run and you refused."

Again, dockhands got us underway. Still trembling as we

headed south into Bogue Sound, I wondered why I'd never seen this side of Tom before. Yes, he'd had bouts of impatience during our years of sailboat charters, particularly in the early years when I seemed to forget much of what I'd learned the year before. Yes, he'd often expressed frustration that I wasn't quicker or stronger. But blaming me for something that wasn't my fault, for something that might well have been his mistake— that was a first! Had he refused to do a dry run because he didn't quite know what to do?

For the second time in less than 10 days, I found myself questioning Tom's judgment. Less than four weeks into our five-year-long adventure, I wanted to go home, but I had no home to go to.

CHAPTER 3

CHOPPY WATERS

WE picked Charleston as our first large urban port of call. A major seaport with ready access to marine supplies and skilled technicians, it seemed an ideal place to work through the long list of boat projects that had to be completed before we could go to sea. I fell in love with it from that first night, as our weary footsteps echoed on the planks of the dark wooden dock at Ashley Marina. The golden glow of the city on one side, the blinking channel lights along the seawall on the other, enchanted me.

But the love affair went on hold the next morning when the rain began. For days, it poured nonstop. The suffocating humidity nurtured layers of mold everywhere, velvety green on varnished teak bulkheads, sooty black on clothes, towels and bedding. I spent hours cleaning each day, only to find a new crop of mold the next morning. The diesel engine grew ever more temperamental. Tom would get it running smoothly one day, only to have it sputter and cough to a stop the next. Many nights we went to bed with the to-do list longer than when we'd awakened that morning.

The weather made both of us grumpy. For the first time in all the years I'd known him, Tom didn't wake up with a smile. Given my history of periodic depression, Tom's morning smile played a far more important role in my life than the simple pleasure of being married to a good humored man. Deprived of that smile, I found myself bursting into tears at the smallest provocation—burnt toast or a sliver in my finger.

And we squabbled constantly over the most ridiculous things, in a way we'd never done in New York. Take, for example, the fuss over the seacocks.

From the aft cabin, where I sat measuring and cutting wood for shelves, I could hear Tom banging around the cockpit. When he came below, he sounded grouchy, "The engine died. I've got to open it up again. I want you to start installing the seacocks."

I looked up, trying to hold my tape measure in place. "I'm a little busy right now. Besides, I know nothing about seacocks. If they aren't done right, the boat could sink."

"Goddammit, can't you do anything anymore?" Tom retorted, his voice harsh. "You've gotten *sooo* lazy since we left New York."

I stood up and began to stomp around the saloon. "Have you noticed," I said, pointing to the bulkheads, "the new light fixtures." I nodded toward the portholes, "and what about the awnings I made, so we can get some air in here when it's raining."

I was on a roll. "And in case you haven't noticed, I've cleaned up the daily crop of mold, shopped for groceries, cooked meals and done laundry."

"You just don't get it, do you?" Tom said, his voice dripping scorn. "We're supposed to be getting ready to go to sea."

"Really??" I replied with sarcasm. "Last I looked, all my tasks were on our to-do list." I paused, for effect. "Well, maybe groceries and laundry aren't on the list. Perhaps you'd prefer me to stop doing those."

Tom scowled. "You know what I mean."

"No, Tom," I said in all seriousness, "I don't have a clue."

"Mary, there's a difference between building shelves and installing the seacocks. We can't go to sea without the seacocks."

"I know that." I said archly. "But we can't go to sea until we can stow all the boxes…for which we need shelves. I'm doing what I know how to do. You're doing what you know how to do. It'll all get done."

Wondering if the engine problems explained his bad temper, I changed tacks. "Hey, sweetie," I said, hoping to placate him, "when I'm done with the shelves, I'll take a look at the seacocks. But not today." I went back to my shelves.

Another fight—one of our silliest—sprung up about water. Tom happened by as I washed lunch dishes.

"Mary, don't run the water like that. You're wasting it. Use the foot pump to rinse stuff."

I gave him a goofy grin, assuming he was making a joke. With mock sarcasm, I said "We're on a dock, hooked up to city water."

"Mary, it's not a laughing matter. You need to learn to conserve water on a boat."

I could feel the heat rising up my neck. My voice came out shrill. "We've been sailing for 12 years and never run out of water. I know perfectly well how to conserve it. But we're on a dock and I'm going to take advantage of it…just like you did while you cleaned the tools this morning!"

He flushed, embarrassed. He'd obviously forgotten about that. As he clambered up to the deck, I wondered once again what he was really annoyed about. I was pretty sure it wasn't my wasting water.

When the rain finally stopped, we explored Charleston on our bicycles, small fold-up affairs designed to fit into a deck locker. Nearly every day thereafter, we made the 10 minute trip to the open air market in the heart of the city to buy fruit, vegetables and fresh fish. Several times a week, we rode through the historic neighborhoods, around the South and East Battery and along the sea wall.

Charleston charmed me, with its small-city scale, its antebellum architecture, its gracious people. A voyeur at heart, I was fascinated by the ornate mansions opened for charity tours in the pre-holiday period, with their high-ceilinged, frescoed ballrooms, lushly planted courtyards and still-used servant quarters. Central Charleston, on the National Register, offers an historic district with period details lovingly preserved. Strolling by a glossy, black iron hitching post, lifting a solid brass knocker on a burgundy and ivory paneled door, meandering across a courtyard cobbled with pale orange brick meant stepping back to another era.

I also liked having family in the area. We frequented the hot tub and the outdoor bar at my cousin Tim's palatial home overlooking the ICW south of Charleston. Tom's Aunt Grace often invited us to dinner at her elegant apartment in the center city. Both generously lent us cars for weekend expeditions to nearby seaside communities. We toured the South Carolina countryside, following mile after mile of the straight highways that ran between rows of loblolly pines to Aiken, where my mother lived. One gorgeous Sunday, Tim gave us a guided tour of the Ashley, Cooper and Wando Rivers on his powerboat, offering us a whole new perspective on the city's waterfront. Grace was a constant source of information on what to see and do.

Tom chatted up all the cruisers he met around the marina,

and we soon had an active social life. We shared many lunches and dinners, sometimes on board one of our boats, sometimes in one of the fine restaurants in town. From time to time, we went to a concert or a play. Except for the humidity, Charleston suited me perfectly...large enough to be interesting and small enough to get around easily.

As I look back on those weeks, I'm amazed we enjoyed Charleston as much as we did, with life on board *Salieri* so grim. Our easy social demeanor with friends and family reflected more than just putting on a good face. The tension seemed to disappear as soon as we got off the boat.

On board, we continued to squabble. There was the kafuffle, one brutally hot day in October, about refrigeration. I'd made three trips to the ice machine outside the marina office. *Salieri* had two airtight lockers in the galley, but refrigeration had never been installed. Having read so many horror stories of cruisers who lost their food supply when the engine or the cooling system failed, I'd planned menus that didn't require refrigeration. But we liked a cold drink on a hot day. I wanted to save leftovers. For that, we needed some cold storage.

As I lugged my third 20-pound bag of ice down the companionway, Tom sat at the saloon table, nursing the last of the cold beer and studying Morse Code. Practicing for his ham radio license exam the following week, his fingers tapped out the dots and dashes on the practice key pad.

As I shoved the bag of ice into the locker, I said, half in jest, "Hey, I have a great idea."

Tom didn't look up. "Ummh?"

"Let's put refrigeration in while we're here. Lugging ice is a pain in the butt and it's gonna get worse as we go farther south."

"You mean you want me to put in refrigeration." Tom continued tapping.

"Well...I'll help, but I don't know anything about refrigeration."

He looked up, clearly annoyed at the interruption. "I'm not going to put in refrigeration."

"Tommmmm...." I said in mock petulance.

"No." He went back to tapping out Morse Code. Even though my initial comment had started out as a joke, I was furious at his refusal to even discuss it. I stashed the ice in the locker and stormed out.

And the set-to over cockpit cushions. I was excited when I got back to *Salieri* after a morning of errands. "Tom, guess what? I found an upholstery shop that'll make us custom cockpit cushions for less than $200. They're dense foam that won't absorb water. And we can get them in bright red to match the sail covers."

He looked up as I came in, but his hands never left the computer keyboard. "We don't need custom cushions. We'll buy a few more of the square float cushions, like the ones we've got."

"Tom, those things are rock-hard and slide all over the place." I paused, hearing the whine in my voice. More calmly, I said, "I don't want to spend the next five years fighting to keep a cushion under my butt every time the boat heels."

Typing once again, he said, "Well, we can't afford $200."

His response surprised me. In New York, we'd rarely disagreed on how much to spend or what to spend it on, but in those days we'd lived well below our means. Now, living off savings, I recognized that if we spent more today, we'd have less tomorrow. But after only six weeks, our cruising budget was little more than an educated guess.

"Who put you in charge of what we can afford?" My voice sounded shrewish. "You spent $1,000 more than we budgeted for the windlass. I trust your judgment. Why don't you trust mine?

"Because you don't seem to realize what it takes to maintain this boat. We won't have the money for the boat if you keep spending it on cockpit cushions or concert tickets."

His reply left me nearly speechless. "Gee, Tom, it would be awful to run out of money after three years. But it would be even worse to spend five years hoarding our money and not enjoy the experience."

Before Tom could respond, I hopped up onto the dock, shouting back as I tromped off, "Your damn float cushions will cost at least $100. An extra $100 to be comfortable for five years hardly seems extravagant." I trudged up to the phone in the marina office and placed the order.

By the end of a month, the SatNav, the windvane, ham radio, single sideband radio, and windlass had been installed. I'd finished all the shelving, varnished the teak bulkheads, and made a cockpit awning. *Salieri* was almost ready to go to sea.

I wasn't. We continued to squabble. We hadn't made love in weeks. Casual conversation seemed a lost art form. Mealtimes, invariably passed in uncomfortable silence, were painful. Where once we had read to each other, we now read our own books to avoid the need to make conversation. Each time I looked up from my book to see Tom buried in his, I wondered how we would survive five years of 24-hour-a-day togetherness if, after only a month, we had nothing to talk about.

One evening in early November, I decided to try to break the tension. I made a show of closing my book and setting it aside.

"Tom," I said. He didn't look up. "Tom," I persisted. When he raised his eyes, I said, as calmly as I could, "We're both so bad-tempered and snippy. We fight all the time. What's wrong?"

His response spilled out, too quickly for him to have given it any thought. "I should think it would be obvious."

Tom's quick retort surprised me. "It's not…so tell me."

He closed his book, his finger marking his place. Glaring at me, he said. "Mary, I feel like I don't know you anymore."

Having no idea what to say, I waited.

He continued. "The woman I married was so capable. You were good at your job. You maintained two houses, your garden, and all the renovations. You probably did more than your share. In all our years in New York, I never worried about how things would get done. They just did."

Without meaning to, I interrupted, "Soooo...what's your point?"

Tom sighed. "All the responsibility for this boat—maintaining it and getting ready to go to sea—has fallen to me. You don't give me any help at all."

"How can you say that? I've done tons of work on the boat. I..."

Tom cut me off. "But not the stuff that makes a boat safe and sound."

I jumped in. "If you mean plumbing and electronics, you're right. I don't know how to do any of it. You always did it in the Berkshires."

Tom retorted, "So, suddenly you can't learn something new? The Mary I married could do anything she wanted to."

"My point exactly, Tom. I *don't want* to. I've never been interested in plumbing or electronics. Why would you expect me to be interested now?"

Tom sat back, his arms folded across his chest, his hands buried in his armpits, his body ramrod stiff. "Because you need to be able to do it."

"Whoooaaa. In all the years we talked about this trip, you never said that my being a mechanic or an electrician came with the deal. The boat's your toy, like the Jaguar. If you need my help, tell me. But I didn't take this trip to become a mechanic."

He leaned forward, glaring at me. "You're right, the Jaguar was a toy. If it didn't run, we had another car and life went on.

But *Salieri* isn't a toy. It's our home and our transportation. You need to know how to take care of it." He paused, "Mary, have you ever asked yourself how you'd manage if something happens to me?"

I sat back, speechless. How could it be, with all the doubts I'd had about the trip, that I'd never asked myself that critical question? My face and neck felt hot. Wondering if they were red, I muttered a reply. "Tom, I've just assumed all along that you'd take care of all the guy stuff. How stupid could a girl be?"

Over fruit and yogurt the next morning, Tom handed me his list of the things he thought I needed to know how to do.

Plumbing (the head and the seacocks)
Setting up the sea-pump
Replacing the hull fittings for the speedo and sonar
Repacking the stuffing box

"Tom, there's only four things on it! I expected a much longer list."

He put his right hand over mine. "Mary, this isn't about a task list, it's about sharing the responsibility. The boat will float even if the engine or the SatNav breaks down. But if a valve fails, we could sink, so we both need to know how to fix it. I wanted you to do the seacocks so you'd learn how they work."

That makes sense, I thought, wishing he'd explained this at the time instead of barking out an order.

I smiled, my first unfeigned smile in several weeks. "I feel pretty dopey." I leaned over and gave him a hug.

"Okay, are you ready for my next list?" His eyes twinkled as he handed me a second piece of paper.

Refrigeration

"I thought you didn't want to put in refrigeration."

"I don't. But nothing says you can't do it."

As I gathered up the breakfast dishes, I realized I knew even less about refrigeration than plumbing. But I could learn. I did a little dance around the galley. *So that's what he's been angry about. Can it really be so easy to solve?*

As agreed, I installed the seacocks and learned how to repair the toilet. I also installed the refrigeration, for which I had to learn to cut stainless steel, solder copper tubing, and pump Freon into the cooling system. I didn't ask for Tom's help on these projects and he didn't offer any.

By the time we left Charleston, we'd established a new equilibrium. I took on more of the burden of managing the boat. Tom had recovered his sense of humor and his wake-up smile. We still struggled to make dinner table conversation, but at least we'd stopped fighting.

CHAPTER 4

SAILING ON THE EDGE

AFTER six weeks tied to a dock, we looked forward to being on the move again. We'd opted for the Atlantic route to Stuart, Florida, rather than the ICW so we could test drive the SatNav, the windvane and our shiny new fishing reel mounted on the stern rail just behind the cockpit. I hoped that three days on the open water would bring Tom and me back in touch again, with each other and with our reasons for taking this trip.

We had one last task, "boxing the compass." With visible landmarks and navigation signals on all sides, Charleston Harbor was a perfect place to check our compass readings against the magnetic headings on the marine chart.

As we slipped the dock lines and powered out of the marina, I felt lightheaded, with even nearby sights and sounds seeming to come from a distance. During two hours of traversing back and forth across the harbor, making small adjustments to the compass on each pass, my skin grew increasingly tender to the touch and I began to shiver. Sounds got ever-more remote, as if I had cotton stuffed in my ears.

By the third and thankfully last hour, I couldn't steer a steady enough course for Tom to confirm the compass readings. When we got back to Ashley mid-afternoon, I crawled into bed and slept through dinner. I slept the whole of the next day, skipping both lunch and dinner.

Excerpt from Salieri's Log (Tom's notes—November 23rd and 24th)

7am Depart Ashley Marina.

8am We're in the Atlantic, heading south. Mary's been hunched up in the cockpit since we raised the sails.

12n Course 180°. The windvane (we've named it "Saf") is steering nicely.

Mary's acting weird. She's still in the corner of the cockpit...has hardly moved in nearly four hours. She just stares at me if I talk to her.

7pm Course 180°. Mary didn't want lunch or dinner—hasn't eaten for two days. She doesn't seem sick, but I don't think she's up to taking a watch tonight.

12m Course 180°. Abeam of Savannah, 55 miles offshore. There's a leak in the stuffing box, around the propeller shaft. The bilge is full of water, right up to the floorboards. I've turned the bilge pump on. Except for an occasional trip to the head, Mary hasn't moved from the cockpit. I'm not sure what to do for her.

5am Course 180°. Abeam of St. Simons, 70 miles offshore. The bilge pump alone couldn't handle the water. It took over an hour with the manual sea pump to get the water out. I've had to pump every hour or so since midnight. I'm exhausted. I have to get Mary to help, somehow.

I sat cross-legged on the cabin floor, bathed in sunlight and working the long stainless steel lever of the sea pump back and forth through a wide arc. Water gushed through the six-inch black plastic tube that snaked out a porthole. Beads of sweat covered my arms, chest and face.

Tom lolled on the settee, his head on the back cushion, his eyes closed. I groaned dramatically, "Man, what a bore. Where'd all this water come from?"

Tom opened his eyes, but didn't move. "We've got a leak. I think it's the stuffing box. It's too much water for the bilge pump, so I've set up the sea pump."

"You're kidding. When did it start?"

"Dunno. But at midnight the bilge was full to the floor-boards. I've been pumping 10 or 15 minutes every hour."

I stopped pumping, trying to get my bearings. "Midnight? What time is it now?"

Tom came and sat on the settee next to me. He stroked my hair. "6:30 in the morning."

"That doesn't make sense…we left at 7 this morning."

"No, hon, we left yesterday morning." He continued to wind his fingers through my hair.

I swung around and looked up at him. "You're kidding. I've lost a whole day. What happened?"

"I wish I knew. You sat huddled in the cockpit from the time we left the dock until I dragged you down here about an hour ago to work the pump."

As I started to work the lever again, I noticed the dark circles under Tom's eyes. "You look exhausted," I said, scanning his face.

"No problem. As long as you're okay. How do you feel?"

"I'm awesomely hungry, but otherwise okay."

"Want me to fix you something to eat?"

"No, thanks. I'll do it once I get the bilge dry. You get some sleep."

"You talked me into it. I'm pooped." Going forward, he turned when he reached the cabin door. "I love you," he said, blowing me a kiss as he closed the door.

Basking in the morning sun, I smiled at the spontaneity of Tom's airborne kiss. He hadn't been so tender in months, maybe even in years. Never particularly demonstrative, Tom's gestures of affection had often seemed scripted, the kind of thing a husband is supposed to do, rather than a response to, or a trigger for, an intimate moment. Now, with the memory of his hands moving through my hair, I felt aglow, close to Tom in a way I hadn't in a very long time.

When I had the bilge pumped dry, I brewed a pot of coffee, mixed some cranberry muffins, and read the log to see what I'd missed. Tom's description of my behavior puzzled me. I remembered being spacey the day before we'd left, but I certainly didn't feel sick now. And the symptoms he described didn't fit the flu or a bad cold.

After noodling it for several hours, I recalled a dinner table conversation in which my mother, a psychiatric social worker, described a patient having an anxiety attack. Her description matched Tom's log. But that didn't answer my question. I'd never had an anxiety attack and, given my sailing experience, I thought it unlikely to have been triggered by a fear of the open water. If it was an anxiety attack, would it happen again? And why?

The leak worsened as the day wore on. By noon, we had to pump at least half of every hour. Rather than going direct to

Stuart, we tucked into Cape Canaveral. In less than two hours, Tom repaired the stuffing box and we were on our way again.

December 9th, my 41st birthday, dawned as a perfect day for a sail.

We were en route to Hawk's Cay, an upscale resort with a deepwater marina where we planned to celebrate an early Christmas with my family. A few miles out of Miami, we caught and cleaned a three-pound snapper. When we anchored for the night, Tom went windsurfing while I made sushi and salad. From the galley, I watched him fly around the bay, skimming over water tinted red-gold from the late afternoon sun. The sight of him, a novice sailboarder, pushing the envelope once again, made me smile. But I noted that the wind, blowing from shore, carried him to the outer reaches of the bay and I wondered, as I cut up tomatoes, exactly what I would do if he got too far downwind and couldn't get back. How would I even know he needed help?

He did get back, of course, and the next day we continued south. As we traveled, we decorated *Salieri* for our first Christmas without snow. I'd brought many of our favorite Christmas ornaments, those that wouldn't break or rust. We lit pine-scented candles, put on a Christmas tape and drank eggnog as we hung the little brass angels from our trip to Munich, the tiny wooden airplanes from Tom's family tree, the multi-colored balls of ribbon that had been a gift from my brother.

Mid-afternoon, we reached the buoy that marked our turn west toward Hawk's Cay. According to the chart, the approach to the marina entrance, itself only a narrow gap in a stone breakwater, had been dredged through a welter of coral heads in very shallow water and marked with six small stakes, three red and three green.

With 15–20 knots of wind from the east, short, steep waves rolled up under our stern as soon as we turned west. *Salieri* surged forward each time she slid down the face of a wave. With both the wind and waves behind us, the boat slewed erratically. It'll be tricky, I thought, to control our motion as we enter the narrow channel.

My temples throbbed. "Should we aim north of the marina entrance?" I asked. "If we drop the sails a quarter-mile out, we can power along the breakwater until we see the stakes."

"No," Tom said airily, "We'll have plenty of time to drop the sails once we see the stakes." He grinned happily. "I don't want to waste a single moment of this gorgeous day. I've got a good bearing on the marina entrance from here. We'll be fine."

I persisted. "Tom, everyone says the stakes are hard to see until you're right on top of them. And you're assuming almost pinpoint accuracy on something that's eight miles away! Do you think it's safe to sail all the way in?"

Like a parent humoring a pestering child, Tom replied evenly. "You're being silly. There's nothing to worry about."

I may be wrong, but I'm not silly. The throbbing intensified, from indignation as much as anxiety. "Okay, do it your way," I spit out. "I'm going below to read."

Determined not to say another word until we were tied up at the dock, I stomped below and slumped on the settee, staring at the chart as if I could maneuver us between those red and green stakes by force of will. The muscles in my legs and back flexed as *Salieri* flew up and down the waves. I stoked my anger by reminding myself, repeatedly, that this was a risk we didn't need to take.

An hour and a half later, Tom called me to come on deck. A quarter mile ahead, two large red metal cans floated parallel to the huge breakwater. The depth sounder read 12 feet.

"See, Mary, we're right on course." He sounded smug.

It didn't look right—*where are the stakes?*—but I concentrated on turning *Salieri* into the wind so Tom could douse the sails. When they were down, Tom pointed to the cans. "Leave them about 15 yards to starboard."

Even with bare poles, *Salieri* continued to skid across the waves. Over the pounding of my heart, I could hear a man's shrill voice on the VHF radio. I couldn't make out what he was saying.

"Tom, are you sure this is right? Where are the red and green stakes...don't red cans mark hazards...why aren't there any green cans...where's the gap in the breakwater...why are there breaking waves ahead of us?"

Tom, on the cabin top furling the mainsail, glared down at me. "Gees, Mary, give it a rest. This is a big resort and I'll bet they've upgraded the entrance. The cans are right where the stakes are supposed to be."

Tom seemed so certain. Was I wrong about the cans? I steered where he'd indicated. Even so, I stopped breathing as the depth sounder dropped...9.0...7.0...6.5.

Suddenly, we slammed to a halt. A lifetime passed as a wave lifted 23,000 pounds of fiberglass and teak and dropped us back onto the sandbar. It happened again. The next wave drove *Salieri* further aground.

Suddenly the screaming voice on the radio penetrated my consciousness. "*Salieri...Salieri...come in, Salieri!!!*"

Tom grabbed the VHF mike. "This is...uh...uh...*Salieri*." His hand trembled.

The voice came back. "Where the hell are you going? Didn't you see the red hazard cans?"

I could see Tom's whole body shaking. "Don't they mark the entrance to Hawk's Cay?"

Another thud. My back and leg muscles started to cramp. A lifetime passed before the voice said evenly, "The entrance is to your right, about four o'clock."

We both turned. There, barely 50 yards away, we saw three red and three green stakes. We'd sailed right past them.

Tom turned back to the mike. "I see it. Is there someone who can pull us off the bar?"

Another thud shook the boat. The voice came back. "Your best bet is to put an anchor out at 45 degrees from your port bow. Can you do that?"

"Yeah, I think so."

"Okay. Pull yourselves up on your anchor and head out in the same direction. You'll be off sooner than if you call a salvage service."

"Thanks. *Salieri* out."

In the steep seas, the dinghy bounced madly, frustrating our efforts to mount the outboard engine and feed the spare anchor onto the dinghy floor. Tom ferried the anchor out as far as the 200-foot line would allow. I watched from the foredeck, each thud reverberating through the soles of my feet. I wondered if the vibration would change if *Salieri* started to break apart.

When Tom had clambered back on board, we began the tedious process of kedging off. As each wave lifted us, I gunned the engine and Tom cranked like mad on the anchor windlass. For eons, our efforts seemed futile, at best halting our shoreward drift. Finally, *Salieri* began to lurch forward, three or four feet at a time.

By the time we had pulled ourselves off the sandbar, dusk had turned to dark. Barely able to see the red and green markers in the graying light, we finally made it through the break-water and tied up at the dock by 7 p.m. Despite the constant pounding on the hard sand, the bilge was dry and the hull was undamaged.

God watches over fools, I thought to myself.

Once the adrenaline rush dissipated, a wave of exhaustion mixed with anger, frustration and embarrassment washed over me. Tom seemed more composed than I felt, but said nothing of any consequence to me that evening. His silence came as a relief. If we talked, I feared I'd say something I'd regret later. I gobbled down some cheese and crackers and went to bed. As I fell asleep, I could hear the clicking of the computer keyboard.

We spent much of the next day doing Christmas shopping and boat errands. Whenever we found ourselves in the same space, the air bristled with tension. I couldn't stop thinking about the grounding. It shouldn't have happened. I wondered, not for the first time, how many of the other mishaps had been of our own making.

I wanted to blame Tom, his unrelenting urge to sail full tilt, his willingness to stake our safety on finding a tiny target in a large sea of shallow water. This was the all-too-familiar dark side of his sense of adventure. For years, I'd lived in fear of dying in the passenger seat of his car. A very skilled driver, Tom was outrageously aggressive on the road, oblivious to the fact that most drivers didn't have his skill. Now, it seemed I might die on his boat.

It was also easy to blame his abrupt—well rude, really— dismissal of my concerns, his refusal to treat me as half of a team. Had we paralleled the breakwater under power until we saw the stakes, it wouldn't have happened. Had we turned around when the markers didn't match the charts, it wouldn't have happened. Each time I replayed the scene, each time I heard again the impatience in his voice, each time I felt the shock of being called "silly," my rage was rekindled.

But as I replayed the scene, I knew I was at fault as well. My response to his rudeness, to his lack of concern had been petulant and childish, much the way I'd always reacted to my mother. To avoid her mockery, I kept my opinions to myself and my form of resistance, such as it was, meant retreating to my room, calling her ugly names from the safety of a place where she couldn't hear me. By retreating below deck, by leaving Tom to sail single-handedly, by cursing him under my breath while saying nothing, I'd abdicated my share of the responsibility for our safety.

I revisited the minutes before the grounding again and

again. Given our obvious inability to work as a team, we would be mad to take *Salieri* offshore into even more challenging conditions.

As I thought about calling off the trip, I recalled my anxiety attack as we left Charleston. Suddenly, I understood that it hadn't been triggered by my fear that something would go wrong. No, it had been triggered by a fear that the shakedown cruise would go *well*, that I'd be committed to sailing around the world with Tom. Sitting in the beauty shop at Hawk's Cay, I came face to face with the realization that I no longer trusted Tom's judgment. And perhaps as important, I didn't like the way he treated me—or the way I treated him—when we were on the boat.

It seemed the cruise had come to a sad end. Could our marriage survive? Could I survive the next 10 days, trying to juggle a failing marriage and a family from which I felt remote?

CHAPTER 5

ALL AHEAD DEAD SLOW

I breathed a huge sigh of relief, mid-morning a week later, as my brother Hugh drove away from the resort hotel with his wife Jeanne, his two girls and my mother in tow. As Tom and I made our way wordlessly through the hotel's manicured gardens, back to the marina, we walked far enough apart that our hands and arms wouldn't touch, even accidentally. Out of the corner of my eye, I watched Tom's carefree stride, his bright yellow polo shirt, his deck shoes without socks—the image of a preppy for whom all was right with the world. Can he really be so oblivious? I wondered.

The vacation had gone far better than expected, mostly because of Hugh's two energetic, platinum-haired daughters. Katie, age four, was a spunky little person who demanded one's attention in an amiable but nonnegotiable sort of way. Jenni, eight months and just learning to walk, had an instinct for stealing center stage. As we worked our way through dolphin shows, a day sail on *Salieri,* and the exchange of Christmas gifts,

50

the two girls provided a consistently entertaining cover for the lack of any genuine affection any of us felt for my mother.

The girls also provided cover for Tom and me. In the week since our near disaster, we'd played out an elaborate charade, that of the loving couple on the cusp of an extraordinary adventure. We hadn't told my family about the accident. I hadn't observed a single break in Tom's indefatigable good humor. I too had played my role well, despite being constantly on the verge of tears as I juggled successive waves of anger, frustration and disappointment.

Under the cover of family activities, however, I'd spent a lot of time reexamining our relationship. Knowing that no marriage is perfect, I had always emphasized Tom's integrity and sense of responsibility and avoided thinking about his willingness to take unacceptable risks. I appreciated his enthusiasm for new adventures and new projects and ignored the fact that most of the tasks we worked on together, particularly during the Berkshire renovations, invariably ended in harsh words and hurt feelings. For years, I gave thanks for his sense of humor and morning smile, and made excuses for him when he showed little interest in the emotional landscape of our marriage. Even when things were going well, I rarely had the sense of Tom reaching out to me, emotionally or sexually.

In truth, over the years, I'd often felt unbearably lonely. More than once, when his aloofness and disinterest had been particularly hurtful, I retreated to the bathroom, where I sat hunched up on the floor of the shower, hoping the noise of the hot running water would cover the sound of my sobs. Even more often, I got through a day only by reaching out for the emotional support of friends who would celebrate my highs and comfort me in my lows. One of my greatest fears about the sailing voyage—that I could not cope if Tom was my only emotional ballast—seemed to have come true.

As we neared the marina, I swallowed hard and said,

"Tom, I'm going back to New York once we get *Salieri* into a berth in Marathon."

"Really...what for?" He didn't look up. From his tone, I wondered if he'd been listening.

"I'm jumping ship."

Now, he turned toward me, his look puzzled, but he kept walking. "Why?"

"You really don't know?" My voice rose in pitch.

"I assume you're upset about the grounding. But, Mary, we had no damage...there's no reason to change our plans for Florida and the Bahamas."

His response stunned me. *He cares more about our travel schedule than about our relationship.* A decade earlier, during a rocky patch in our young marriage, I'd felt a similar need for space. "Tom," I'd said in a calm voice, "I'm going to get a room in the Barbizon for a while. I want a little time to myself."

"You're joking" he'd replied with obvious disbelief. "Mary, we're leaving for St. Lucia next week to go sailing."

"I don't care about St. Lucia. Right now, I need to think about what I want from this marriage."

"But we'll lose our deposit if we cancel now."

I'd laughed because otherwise I would have cried. But over the next few days, he convinced me that the vacation would be a time for us to talk, to work out the kinks. And so, I'd stayed. Things did improve and yet...years later, I still wanted to cry.

Instead, I took a deep breath. "Tom, I don't give a damn about Florida or the Bahamas. I'm so angry that..."

Tom broke in. "Mary, I made a mistake last week. I should have known the cans were wrong. You don't have to beat me up about it."

It was a first, his admitting he'd made a mistake. But the cans were the least of it. The real mistake was sailing eight miles in when we didn't know the area and the sea conditions were against us. "...you take such unnecessary risks. I'm angry that you discount every opinion I offer. And..."

He stopped and grabbed my upper arm as he interrupted again. "I don't discount your opinions. I have a lot of respect for you. I always have."

"You don't act like it. If you'd taken my suggestion, we wouldn't have gone aground."

Tom glared at me. "Okay, so this time you were right. But I get so tired of your worrying because you don't understand sailing dynamics."

I glared back. My words came out like bullets. "And I get so tired of being scared because I don't understand what you're trying to do, because I don't have the strength or agility to respond quickly if something goes wrong."

He started walking again. I continued. "Tom, maybe my ideas don't always make sense, but they're sure as hell not silly. It's not acceptable to do what you want to do simply because you think you know better."

"Mary, I made a mistake. But, Jesus, it's not the end of the world."

With a jolt, I realized we were having two different conversations. He wanted to talk about the details of the accident and I wanted to talk about our inability to work as a team. Shrugging my shoulders, I said, "It's not just this one mistake. It's three months of mistakes, three months of being scared. I don't want to live this way."

We reached *Salieri*. As I climbed aboard, Tom stopped on the dock.

"Mary, I forgot to call Brewer's to check on a part for the windlass." He turned back toward the hotel, waving amiably, as if we'd been chatting about a movie or a book. "Don't wait lunch."

I watched him walk away, amazed at his jaunty stride. If it wasn't sincere, he was putting on a marvelous act. If it was, he was a monster. Whichever, his departure seemed so typical, a standard maneuver to avoid a tough conversation.

But I was also relieved to have a little time to myself. I

attacked some housekeeping chores that didn't require much concentration. When I had changed the sheets, washed the dishes and cleaned the bathroom, I fixed a plate of cheese and fruit and sat down at the computer to print out Christmas letters, another mindless task.

Tom returned mid-afternoon. Uncharacteristically, he came below without a greeting and slumped on the settee directly across from me, staring into the middle distance. I ignored him.

After a few minutes, he spoke, his voice a whisper. "Mary, please don't go back to New York. I don't know exactly what I need to do differently, but I want this trip to work for both of us."

I looked up. He looked sad, like a puppy that had just been scolded. But his sadness wasn't enough. "I have to think about it. We'll talk when we get to Marathon." I returned to my letters.

We left the next afternoon for Boot Key in Marathon. At breakfast the following morning, Tom asked, "Have you decided about New York?"

"No."

"When will you decide?"

"I don't know," I said irritably. I didn't like being pressured

"Mary, I don't want you to go." Tom leaned across the table and wrapped both his hands around mine. "Can we talk about what happened when we went aground?"

That took me by surprise. Tom wasn't the sort to start difficult conversations. "Okay. You start."

Tom hesitated. "Mary, you accused me of not listening to

you. I think I've gotten into a bad habit." He paused, as if he were looking for the right words. "I think we both have."

I waited.

"I've always had trouble figuring out when you have an opinion and when you're just floating a trial balloon. You never start a sentence with 'I want...' Instead, you always ask a question—'should we...' or 'why don't we...' or 'do you want to...'"

I could feel the knot forming in my stomach.

He continued, "I can't tell you how many times I've realized—waaaaay too late—that you weren't asking a question, that you were really telling me what you wanted. Each time it happens, I swear I won't make that mistake again. But I do. I keep falling into the same old trap."

He sat back, one arm along the back of the settee. "Oddly enough, it's 'cuz I do respect you. I know you can express yourself just fine when you want to. So when you ask me a question, I instinctively assume you mean it as a question."

His voice was tentative when he spoke again. "That's what happened last week. You asked if we should be more cautious. I said 'no.' You asked again, different words but the same question. You kept asking. After a while, I did stop listening."

I got up from the table and put my cereal bowl in the sink, feeling a need to put some space between us. "That's a cop-out. If you have so much respect for me, why didn't you try to understand my concern before you said no?"

Tom's retort was emphatic. "It **is not** a cop-out. You asked me what I wanted to do. I told you. You never said, "I don't agree." In fact, as I recall, you said 'okay, do it your way.'"

He paused, and then continued forcefully. "Mary, you can't expect me to read your mind."

At those words, I flashed back to an afternoon when, at eight or nine years of age, I'd arrived home from school to find my mother standing by the front door in a rage.

"Where on earth have you been? I've been waiting for you

for nearly an hour." Her face was flushed. I steeled myself for whatever was to come.

"I stopped for a Coke with Carolyn and Toni, like every day."

"Mary, I came home to take you shopping for shoes." She grabbed my shoulders and shook me. It didn't hurt, but I was frightened. "I don't have time to wait around for you to show up whenever you feel like it."

"I didn't know you wanted to buy shoes today. You didn't say anything this morning about coming home early from work."

"I didn't know then. But my 3:30 appointment got cancelled."

"How was I supposed to know that?" I whined.

"Don't be lippy with me, young lady. Go to your room, right now."

Alone in my bedroom with the afternoon sun playing on the lavender walls, I tried to figure out how I could have known she wanted me home early. I wondered how I could learn to read her mind. This scene, with small variations, played itself out a thousand times during my childhood.

Omigod, you're doing to Tom what your mother so often did to you.

I could see Tom waiting for a response. Finally, I said, "I never saw that pattern before. You're right, I need to think about doing a better job of letting you know what I want."

Over the next 24 hours, I pondered my unwillingness—or maybe inability—to tell Tom what I thought or what I wanted. Clearly, it was unfair to saddle Tom with baggage I carried from my childhood. But learning to speak my mind wouldn't alter my unwillingness to spend the next few years living scared. The following evening, during dinner, I broached the subject.

"Tom, it drives me crazy when you take risks we don't need to take."

Tom stared into his wine glass. I waited.

Eventually, with obvious hesitation, he spoke, without looking up. "Mary, I've been racing since I was a kid, first on Lake Michigan, then on Long Island Sound. It's all I know how to do."

"Tom, we're not on a race. Why can't you just be good at cruising?"

Tom leaned forward. He sounded earnest. "I don't know how to sail 'sort of.'"

I sensed an impasse. "Tom, I'm not going to spend the next five years feeling like catastrophe is just past the next buoy. If you want me to stay, you'll have to learn to sail more cautiously."

Neither conversation resolved anything, but we were finally beginning to confront conflicts that had been latent for years. Hoping that the voyage on *Salieri* had finally launched us on the road to emotional intimacy, I stayed.

.

PART II

LEARNING TO NAVIGATE

CHAPTER 6

THE WIND AT OUR BACK

W E dallied in Marathon, Florida, a month longer than planned. The Florida Keys appealed to us far more than we'd expected and we whiled away many delightful days exploring the chain of islands by car and by boat, with friends or by ourselves. We made daytrips to Key West for shopping, movies or dinner and learned to scuba dive in the coral-strewn waters of Hawk Channel. And last but not least, we took the opportunity in Marathon, a major port of call for long-term cruisers, to take copious notes on what to do and where to go once we were cruising offshore.

In truth, we also dallied because neither of us was quite ready to sever the ties that had nurtured us for 40 years. Leaving Marathon would take us into foreign waters, not just physically, but emotionally, socially and culturally. All the doubts that had been voiced in the months before we left New York, along with some we hadn't thought of then, now bubbled to the surface. Could we cope without friends and family? What if we didn't speak the language? Did we have enough food? Did we have the right combination of foods? Would our navigation skills be adequate in offshore waters, where nautical guides were less reliable than in the U.S.? Would we be motivated to keep going when there was no place we had to be and no one who cared when we arrived? Would we get bored?

And then, of course, we were deterred by the still-painful memory of crashing and banging our way down the ICW. The months in Marathon had done little to forge us into a team. With so many distractions—old friends who came to visit, new friends to learn from—we'd gone back to living parallel lives. As in New York, Tom and I shared stories and compared notes on a daily basis and 'made a date' when we wanted to do something specific together.

On the positive side of the ledger, we rediscovered what we'd once found interesting in one another and dinner conversations came easily. On the negative side, we were no closer to knowing whether we could depend on each other when we were all we had.

I wondered if the Bahamas, our next destination, was the right place to test our team skills. The appeal of the islands was obvious...water as clear as the air itself, colorful coral easy to see, sheltered anchorages with good holding, scuba diving reputed to be among the best in the world.

The risks were equally apparent. The Bahamian islands, all 260,000 square miles of them, lay in a patchwork of rocky outcrops—shallow, coral-infested banks—with deep ocean trenches that vary from several hundred to several thousand feet. When the tide runs, fierce currents can sweep a sailboat miles off course. When the northeast wind blows without interruption for 4,000 miles across the Atlantic and bumps up against the Bahama Banks, it generates short, steep waves that can drive an unwary sailboat onto a rocky shore in the two seconds it takes to check the depth sounder. I took some comfort from the knowledge that we'd be checking in daily to the "ham net," a scheduled confab of cruisers who were also ham radio operators. At least, I reassured myself, someone will know where we are.

As departure day inched closer, I hoped Tom and I had learned to appreciate our different styles and different needs, not just in the abstract, but in the right-here-and-right-now. *Will we get it right before disaster strikes again?*

We pulled away from the dock at Boot Key a little after noon toward the end of February 1986. As we made our last trip out through the lush mangrove-lined channel, Tom had the helm, his even more faded orange-and-yellow hat shielding his balding head from the blazing Florida sun. Manatees cavorted among the roots of the trees. Pelicans sat stolidly on the wooden pilings, waiting for the right moment to pluck lunch from the water. Raucous frigate birds were everywhere, flying madly about, hitting the water like torpedoes when they saw fish. Through it all, white ibis stood by like pieces of sculpture, regally taking it all in.

As the channel life passed by, I scrolled through scenes from our months in Marathon. We'd spent a marvelous week sailing to the Dry Tortugas and back with the Safirsteins, good friends from my graduate school days, who came with their three daughters to help close this chapter of our life. Friends who came to visit in their four-seater plane gave us an afternoon tour, a bird's eye view of the deep water channels and sandy shoals—including the sandbar at Hawk's Cay—that had taken us weeks to navigate in *Salieri*.

We'd celebrated our wedding anniversary in Key West with an elegant dinner on an ornate wrought iron balcony, watching the setting sun reflected in the tropical water and pleased to have reconnected. Then, too, we whiled away many a lazy evening in penny-ante poker with my Uncle Marvin, legendary in my family for his card-sharking techniques. We always lost but were always ready for the next game. I would genuinely miss Marathon.

In Coffin's Patch, about 10 miles offshore, we met up with two other sailboats en route to the Bahamas. Our little convoy made the 90-mile trip across the Gulf Stream comfortably and we were all safely anchored in the Bimini Islands on the western edge of the Bahama Banks two hours before a nor'easter barreled in with 40-knot winds. While the storm raged around us, Tom and I sat dry and comfortable, if a little bouncy, plotting our course to Nassau.

Our route would take us east, directly across the Bahama Banks, with an overnight stop at Chubb Cay. After laying out the course, I showed it to Tom. "It's a 13-to-15 hour trip. If we start before dawn, we'll have the anchor down in Chubb by sunset. But I don't like dodging coral heads in the dark tomorrow morning."

Tom peered at the chart. "I agree. I'd rather leave at dawn, when we can see the coral. We'll have to anchor at Chubb in the dark, but *Allegro's* made this trip several times. Matt says the lights for Chubb are easy to see from a long way off and the water is deep right up to the anchorage."

I scrunched up my face. "I don't like that idea much either."

"Well, we could always anchor for the night at the edge of the Banks and make the short hop to Chubb the next day."

"Sold." I said with enthusiasm. "Let's leave at first light."

The Banks were far from our first experience with sailing in coral, but the passage across mile after mile of crystal clear water over brilliant white sand felt like floating on air. We kept checking the depth sounder to make sure the water was deep enough for our six-foot draft. In fact, it rarely dropped below 10 feet.

At dusk, the Northwest Channel light on the eastern edge of the Banks appeared as expected. Tom traced out the deep water route to Chubb on the chart. "I'm game to go for Chubb tonight. Whaddya think?"

It had been a lovely day, one I didn't want to end. Feeling a renewed confidence in our sailing skills, I said, "Yeah. Let's go for it."

Tom smiled and gave me a thumbs up. "Cool. The course is 165°, a bit east of south. I bet we'll have the anchor down by 9 o'clock."

Not quite. By 8 p.m., we were in complete darkness, with no navigation lights visible anywhere. Our only reference point, a faint glow on the horizon, lay in the general direction of Chubb.

My shoulders started to ache when Tom came back on deck, frowning. "The SatNav says we've drifted well north of our rhomb line. That's why we don't see any lights. We need to head due south for a while."

An hour later, when the radio beacon for Chubb finally appeared, I breathed a sigh of relief. An hour more and the lights on shore were distinctly visible. Tom unhooked the wind-vane and took the helm. "Mary, do you see the red and green lights for the channel?

I peered through the binoculars. "Nope."

Another half-hour. The shore lights were now menacingly close, but I saw no red or green lights. The water depth dropped fast, from 50 to 30 feet in a boat length. By the time we lowered the sails, we had less than 20 feet of water. With Tom inching *Salieri* forward, I perched on the bow with a high intensity searchlight, beaming it down into the water in front of our bow.

"Tom, the bottom is sand, but there's lots of coral heads." I tried to keep the anxiety out of my voice.

I could see tension lines in Tom's face. "Mary, the water's down to 12 feet. Drop the hook here. I don't know where in hell we are, but I'm not going any closer to those lights."

The anchor grabbed solidly on the sandy bottom. By 11

p.m., we were sound asleep. In the last moments before I dozed off, I smiled to myself. We've passed our first "team test," I thought.

We awoke the next morning to find huge conch lying in the white sand beneath our keel, just waiting to be plucked out for lunch. The entrance to the anchorage lay 20 yards behind us. The red and green stakes marking the entrance were unlit. Had we continued on, we would have hit a solid wall of coral.

The team had it right!

To wrap up the last details on his consulting business, Tom flew back to New York for 10 days. I toyed with the idea of going with him, but decided to stay with *Salieri* in East Bay Marina, a stone's throw from one of Nassau's largest open-air food markets.

The logistics of the tiny marina—several boats invariably had to move whenever one came in or went out—meant that the dozen yacht owners all knew each other. Once the others learned I was alone, they went out of their way to include me in their activities. This unexpectedly comfortable environment offered lots of opportunities for one-on-one conversation, a welcome change from the group socializing I found so difficult. Marina residents came from all over the world and discussion topics ranged from the mundane (how to avoid cockroaches) to the high-minded (Zen philosophy, bio-ethics or international politics).

With companions from the marina, I explored Nassau, not the glitzy Paradise Island of tourist fame, but the historical town and the present-day world of the people who live there. I studied its history as a seafaring and agricultural community. I scoured the bookstores for fiction based on island life and read voraciously. I learned to make seviche (raw fish "cooked" in lime juice), conch fritters (fried dumplings made with furiously pounded conch meat) and cocada (a devastatingly rich concoction of coconut, eggs and sugar). I revarnished the 62-foot-high mast and, as I worked, listened to Berlitz tapes on Spanish, which we'd need in the Dominican Republic and Panama. As part of an idea for a book, I interviewed several midlife cruisers, exploring their motivation for dropping out, the reactions of their families and friends, the changes in their attitudes as the cruise progressed.

I felt content in a way I couldn't ever remember, waking up each morning eager to get about the day, even without the benefit of Tom's smile. Each hour brought a new experience...a vegetable I'd never tasted, music I'd never heard before, recommendations for new books to read. After years of letting Tom take the lead with strangers, it thrilled me to realize I hadn't lost the ability to make new friends. I decided, as the days passed, that this was why I had given up my career to go sailing. My enthusiasm for our cruise grew steadily.

Tom's grumpy mood when he returned came as a shock to my system. As he described his meetings in New York, his tone had an edge of despondency.

"Are you sorry," I asked, "you gave up the business...that you walked away from something so successful?"

"No, not at all," he said, but his voice lacked conviction.

"You seem down...did anything go wrong?

"No, closing the business down went according to plan. I'm just tired," he said irritably. "I'll be fine after a good night's sleep."

I was even less prepared for the apathy with which he greeted my newfound enthusiasm. As I talked about the day-trips I'd taken, the interviews I'd done, the books I'd read, he asked few questions and offered no commentary. He responded politely but without warmth to the friends I'd made in the marina. For a day or two, I made excuses for him, waiting for him to get that good night's sleep. But after several days of his persistent disinterest, I felt like a balloon slowly losing air.

I stopped doing the interviews. I spent increasingly less time on Spanish lessons. For a few days, I clung to the emerging friendships I'd made in his absence, but the vitality seemed to have gone out of them. Several times, in the week after Tom's return, I dreamt about being lost. In one dream, I stood on the dock in the marina calling for help, but I seemed to be invisible and no one could see me.

Something was wrong, and I had no idea what.

Not long after Tom's return, we left for the Exumas, a chain of islands running generally southeast through the center of the Bahamas. With navigation markers often missing, we lived in a state of constant stress. We had more than our share of nail-biting moments as we struggled into or out of an anchorage with strong winds and ferocious currents. My anxiety level spiked each time we heard a radio distress call—often once or twice a day—from a yacht that had gone up on the rocks.

The anchorages weren't much better. Strong currents often made it impossible to swim from *Salieri* for fear of being carried out to sea. Our dinghy, with its tiny 2HP engine, struggled against the wind and currents as we headed to shore or back out again, and we often arrived at our destination both wet and cold. Many of the islands were little more than deserted piles of razor-edged volcanic rock, hard to walk on and devoid of vegetation. Those that were inhabited rarely offered more than an ill-stocked grocery store and a foul-smelling pub.

My gloomy mood leaving Nassau, along with Tom's near-constant state of irritability, undoubtedly colored my perspective on those first weeks. Outgoing and friendly when other yachties were around, he became morose and self-absorbed when we were alone. We didn't fight, but neither did we talk much. I found it hard to read, and when we weren't hiking or snorkeling or making a picnic, I sat at the saloon table playing solitaire—hour after hour of trying to make the cards come out right.

To be fair, we shared many positive moments, strolling along crescent beaches of brilliant white sand at sunrise or sunset. We joined in many nighttime picnics with other cruisers. We snorkeled for hours, gazing with amazement at the purple and yellow and orange coral. We stalked endless schools of tropical fish, learning in the process which ones—grouper, snapper, barracuda—were safe to eat. Tom learned how to spear fish and worked on his sailboarding technique.

Our daytime activities took place under an intensely blue sky, peppered with high white cumulus clouds. The night sky, untainted by ground lights, was dense with stars I'd never seen before. As we navigated the islands, we got things comically wrong a couple of times, but we had no mishaps.

My spirits soared when we arrived in Georgetown, a major port of call in the heart of the Exumas. This picture-book Caribbean village, with houses and shops in a rainbow of pastels, caters to a multinational community. At the Peace & Plenty Hotel or one of the many bars, you could find hamburgers, barbecued goat, pizza or conch fritters. We contributed to nightly potluck picnics on the beach and joined in daily snorkeling expeditions. Nearly every day, we took an island tour to explore the history, architecture and vegetation. We slept soundly in an anchorage free of errant currents.

To my delight, we caught up with cruisers we'd met before, some as far back as Charleston. We met many more who would be traveling with us for months to come, including Jim and Judy Weaver on the magically named *Dream Weaver.* Jim, a high school athlete and an Ohio State diving champion, had been coached for years by my father. Like us, Jim and Judy had come to Georgetown for the Family Island Regatta, a three-day race for traditional Bahamian fishing boats.

The atmosphere grew more festive by the day, as yet another fleet of catboats sailed in. Their clean, crisp lines, with hulls painted in vivid, primary shades of red, blue or green contrasted sharply with frothy whitecaps spattered across the pale aquamarine bay. The color palette expanded further when spectators came out in their orange or yellow dinghies. Hordes of sailboarders—including Tom—with day-glo Mylar sails in chartreuse and fuchsia followed the catboats around the course.

The keel-less catboats, nearly a hundred of them in all, were thrilling to watch as they sped around the race course. The boats balanced the power of their huge sails by propping a long plank out to windward and piling just the right number of crewmembers just the right distance out on the board. If the crew failed to anticipate even a small shift in the wind, the boat would capsize, with the sail suddenly underwater and the crew hurtling into the water on top of it, amid uproarious laughter. With *Salieri* anchored near the starting line and friends at the finish line, we were blessed with ringside seats all three days.

A few days in this magical place drained away the stresses and strains of the previous weeks. Tom's good humor reemerged while my energy level began to rise again. Between island tours, the races and nightly picnics, I restarted the interviews and persuaded Tom to join me in Spanish lessons.

During our two weeks in Georgetown, my body and psyche finally shifted to island time. As we headed out for the next chapter of the voyage, I assured myself that life would be better now that Tom and I had finally settled into the cruiser's life.

And it was. South of Georgetown, the cruising grounds proved more welcoming, with deep water, wide channels and negligible currents. We dawdled for a day on the long, crescent beach at Concepçion Island where, the locals will tell you, Columbus actually landed. We spent several days at Rum Cay, scuba diving on a reef that offered brilliant reds and yellows and lavenders 100 feet down. By the time we began the three-day passage to the Turks & Caicos, an island nation 600 miles southeast of Miami, the cruising life had me hooked.

During this passage, our longest since we'd left New York, we began to adjust to the realities of everyday life on a sailboat. To make sure we did not accidentally drift into the path of a freighter or fishing trawler, we established a watch schedule based on alternating four-hour shifts, both day and night. With no access to supermarkets, I began to make my own bread and grow alfalfa sprouts so we'd always have something fresh. We experimented with different sail combinations, and celebrated with ice-cold beer when we finally figured out how to "heave to," the preferred sail trim for storm conditions.

The highlight of this trip came when we discovered we could use the ham radio to talk to friends and family at home as if we were making a local call, an unexpected thrill in the days before cell phones. Our first call, to my brother, went through a ham radio operator in Denver. I will never forget my brother's response when I said, "Hi, it's Mary."

"Who?" he asked.

"Mary, your sister."

"No, really," he insisted. "She's on a sailboat in the Atlantic. Who is this?"

When I finally convinced him, we talked for nearly half an hour, at no cost to us, and a cost of 10 cents to the ham operator who had patched us through.

Early in the morning on the third day, we turned into the entry channel for the port of Providenciales. Moments later, the VHF radio crackled.

"*Salieri, Salieri*, this is *Dream Weaver.*" I heard Judy's voice.

Grinning ear to ear, I grabbed the mike. "Hi *Dream Weaver*, where are you?"

"In Provo, waiting for you. Let's go to Channel 19."

I switched channels. "*Dream Weaver*, this is *Salieri.*"

"So, how'd your trip go?" That was Roger on *Dancing Lady.*

"Very smooth. Are you in Provo too?"

"Yup," Roger replied. "Right next to *Dream Weaver.* We heard you on the ham net last night and figured you'd be here in time for lunch. There's a nifty bistro in town. Want us to wait for you?"

"Aren't you nice?" I replied, still grinning. "But, we're so pooped we wouldn't be good company. Our first order of business is naps. But we'll see you for dinner."

As I hung the mike on its hook, a wave of warmth washed over me. My delight went far beyond seeing friends after a few days at sea. The sound of familiar voices, the fact of friends awaiting our arrival, signaled that *Salieri* had finally become my home.

Our week in the Turks & Caicos yielded two very powerful images. One came the day before we left. Eating breakfast in the cockpit, Tom and I watched as the 45-foot *Jalan Jalan* prepared to leave. Watching cruisers anchor or depart is a favorite sport of yachtsmen, since so many sailors don't know how to get into or out of an anchorage. We expected a good show, as Bruce, a single-hander, would have to raise the anchor and the sails by himself.

Morning coffee in hand, Bruce strolled forward and gave a brief push on the windlass switch with his toe, just enough to pull the slack out of the anchor chain. Then he went amidships and cranked the mainsail up partway, not enough to catch the wind. He went below. A few minutes later, he came up, coffee cup still in hand. He hit the windlass button again to pull out the slack that had formed in the interim. He went through this routine several more times in the next 10 minutes, always holding that coffee cup, totally unhurried.

When the anchor chain hung straight up and down, holding the yacht in place only by its weight, he cranked the mainsail the rest of the way up. With the sail flapping, he went back to the cockpit and—finally putting his coffee cup down—took the mainsheet in one hand and the helm in the other. He steered *Jalan Jalan* out between us and *Dream Weaver*. That scene reflected the complete integration of man, machine and nature.

Turning to Tom, I asked, "Do you suppose we'll ever be able to do that?"

He laughed. "My racing buddies would never approve of such dawdling. But I don't think we can consider ourselves real cruisers until we can."

I shivered with pleasure. Perhaps Tom had learned to be a cruiser, no longer so determined to sail at the edge.

Another powerful image came the day of our departure. We'd gotten a late start and decided to anchor for the night in the lee of Ambergris, a tiny patch of sand at the southeast corner of the Caicos Banks. From the calm anchorage, we watched Mother Nature put on an awesome show of pyrotechnics—heat lightning around 360 degrees of the horizon. The sky changed from red to white to green and back again for hours without any sign of rain.

It seemed a spectacular omen. The Bahamas and Caicos had been an adventure, but they were American playgrounds where everyone spoke English and sailing charts were reasonably good. Now, as we headed to the Dominican Republic, we would enter an unfamiliar world where we didn't speak the language and knew little about local customs. Our instincts as well as our charts were likely to be unreliable.

It was nice of Mother Nature to give us such a glorious send-off.

On Bruce's recommendation, we opted to go east through

Turk's Passage, an unmarked channel through the three-mile-wide reef between Ambergris and Fish Cay, rather than take the longer but well-marked route around the north end of Fish Cay. As we searched for the pass, whitecaps littered the sea surface under overcast skies. Even from my position strapped on the bow pulpit, it was a challenge to see the random coral heads only a few feet below the surface.

For two hours, I'd been drenched by nearly every passing wave. Fatigue was setting in. I wanted warm tea and dry clothes. I began to panic. *What if I miss seeing a coral head and fail to signal Tom to ease our course to the right or left? What if Tom's attention wanders and he misses a signal?*

I thought about changing places with Tom, back in the cockpit and well-protected from the cold waves. But his task was no easier than mine, as he tried to maneuver us on a nautical slalom course based only on hand signals from me. At least I could see where we were going. He was steering blind and undoubtedly had a fistful of anxiety in his stomach.

Too tired to go on, I was ready to signal Tom to head back toward the main channel when my eye caught a glint of deep blue on the mottled brown surface. Within seconds, it emerged as a wide stripe of sapphire, a glittering path through the dull orange reef. I knew it meant deep clear water over pure white sand.

My heart began to pound. I could only see a quarter-mile ahead. *What if this isn't Bruce's path? What if it's only a rocky cul-de-sac? Is it wide enough for Salieri to turn around if it ends halfway across the reef?*

I wanted Tom's opinion but couldn't leave the bow while we were still in coral-infested water. With the sapphire stripe nearly abeam, I had to make a decision. I swallowed hard and decided to go for it. I signaled to Tom to turn.

Salieri's bow curved to the right. The water between us and the channel was free of coral, but with a full keel, we were slow to turn. Our bow pointed toward the rocky edge of the reef on the north side of the channel. I signaled frantically for Tom to sharpen the turn. Slowly, interminably slowly, the bow came around. As we straightened out in the calm waters of the channel, I could see a carpet of smooth white sand 15 feet below us.

Reassured by the calm blue water unfolding ahead of us, I headed back to the cockpit. For the next hour, storm clouds raced overhead, the wind whistled in the rigging, and waves broke noisily against the reef on either side. *Salieri* flew across the reef.

Tom and I and Mother Nature had learned to work as a team.

CHAPTER 7

SETTING THE STAGE

DIRTY. Dangerous. Unwelcoming to yachties. That's what we'd heard about Panama. We hoped to spend as little time as possible there, topping off provisions, repainting *Salieri's* hull with anti-fouling paint, and transiting the Canal to get to the Pacific Ocean.

However low our expectations, they didn't prepare us for the dismal reality of the Canal Zone on the Atlantic side of the isthmus. Only moments after we'd anchored in the Flats, even before Customs arrived, we heard banging on our hull. When we came on deck, we saw a gaunt, nervous looking fellow with a long, scraggly beard, his shorts riding so low his pubic hair curled over his waistband. His balance, in a wooden dinghy that hadn't had a coat of paint in years, seemed precarious.

"Hi," he said. "I'm Jim. My wife and I are transiting the Canal tomorrow. Would you be interested in being line handlers on our boat?"

We had been advised repeatedly not to take *Salieri* through the Canal until we had experience on other boats. The six locks, each 110-foot wide, are designed for commercial ships that fit snugly between the walls. By contrast, a sailboat with a 12-foot beam has to be secured in the middle of each lock with lines tied, fore and aft, to the "mules," the small locomotives that control each side of the canal.

The challenges cannot be understated. In each lock, with only minutes to spare, the crew has to connect four heavy lines to messenger cables tossed by canal staff on the mules, nearly 50 feet away. In the three up-bound locks, the crew cannot allow slack to form in the lines as the water in the lock rises, since the turbulence can roll a yacht violently enough to break a stay. On the three down locks, we had the opposite problem—if the crew keeps the lines too taut as the water drops, the cleats will tear right out of the deck.

To minimize damage, Canal authorities required every sailboat to have at least seven people on board, including the captain, four line handlers, a pilot employed by the Canal and one spare hand for good measure. Jim wanted us to be two of those seven.

Jim's appearance didn't inspire much confidence, but I didn't know how easy it would be to find other crewing opportunities. I looked at Tom, who cocked his head to indicate he'd go. With considerable trepidation, I said "yes." As Jim rowed off, I wondered what we'd gotten ourselves into.

When we arrived in the appointed place at 4 a.m. the next morning, I was aghast to see what looked more like a raft than a sailboat, low to the water and flat. Aptly named *Mini Boat,* the vessel measured only 18 feet fore to aft, its deck barely large enough to accommodate the seven bodies required for the transit. Jim had never installed lifelines, so the risk of falling overboard was very real. The boat had no head, so anyone who had to pee during the ten-hour trip would have an audience. Sue, his wild-eyed and obviously stoned wife, had not thought of paper plates or plastic cups, so there were not enough dishes for all of us to eat at once.

Still in shock when Miguela, the Canal Pilot, arrived, I watched from the dock as she announced quite firmly, "You can't take this boat through the canal. You don't have the proper equipment."

"Excuse me, *madam,*" Jim said, his tone highhanded. "We have a permit, so we're going."

Miguela stepped on board, looking doubtful, and toured the tiny deck. "You don't have enough cleats or winches to handle four separate lines," she said. "And the ones you have are too small for the size of your lines." Standing near the stern, she pointed to the outboard engine strapped to one of the gunnels. "That engine won't move this boat at five knots." Shaking her head, she said in a firm tone, "You can't transit the Canal unless you can maintain a speed of five knots."

In a shockingly rude gesture, Jim waved his Canal *permiso* in her face. "The officer who inspected us—a man, I might add—said we would be just fine. I can't imagine that you know more about what qualifies for transit than he did."

She recoiled, as if she'd been slapped. I prayed she'd cancel the transit, if only in response to his abominable behavior. My heart sank when she acquiesced.

I cannot imagine a more harrowing experience. With inadequate cleats and winches, the seven of us needed brute strength to control the lines. In the up-bound locks, it was impossible to maintain a constant tension. The boat spun wildly in the turbulence as the locks flooded. In the second lock, when Sue's line suddenly slipped off the single cleat on the bow, she lost her balance and tumbled into the black, oily waters, slipping instantly below the murky surface. If she had slipped under the boat, the hull, swinging erratically, would bash her skull.

In a complete panic, Jim shouted wildly—"find her"…"toss a line to her"…"get her." In fact, we could do little, even if we had been able to see her. With Sue's line now floating in the water, it took all of the crew—including the pilot—to keep some measure of control with the three remaining lines. Eventually,

Sue popped to the surface and crawled back on the deck. Apart from swallowing oily, dirty water, she seemed none the worse for wear.

As predicted, the dinghy engine couldn't do the job, and our expected five-hour trip across Gatun Lake took closer to 10. By the time we arrived at Pedro Miguel, the first down lock on the Pacific side, we had missed our slot by several hours. In desperation, Miguela requested the Canal authorities to let us transit the down locks lashed alongside an official tugboat. Things went smoothly enough until we reached the last lock, where salt and fresh water mix as the gates open. The vertical vortex generated by the mix is powerful enough to swamp a yacht much larger than *Mini Boat*. To avoid getting swamped, a sailboat has to retrieve all its lines and be out of the lock in less than 45 seconds.

The dinghy engine failed us once again, leaving us well inside the lock when the vortex hit. What felt like a wall of water swept over the low deck, making it almost impossible to maintain a solid footing. Holding my breath as the boat pitched, I waited for the metal stay I was hanging onto to break. By the time we had escaped the vortex, my knees would barely hold me up.

During the three-hour bus ride back to Colon, Tom and I imagined all manner of risks in taking *Salieri* through the Canal. We would, we decided, arrange to go through the Canal at least once more before we braved this terrifying journey on our own.

Our view of Panama did not improve by the light of the next day. We'd arranged for a slip at the Panama Canal Yacht Club to get access to laundry facilities and hot showers. To our consternation, we also got a noisy bar patronized primarily by scruffy, hard-drinking sailors and an eight-foot-high chain link fence, locked to protect yachtsmen from any marauding thieves. My heart sank when we learned it would be nearly a month before the boatyard would have space for us to haul *Salieri* and repair her bottom. I was close to tears, a few days later, when we awoke to find a thick ring of yellow-black sludge from an oil spill coating several inches of our lovely ivory hull.

Our first expedition into the nearby town of Colon for food and supplies depressed us even more. Walking around the streets, we found unrelenting dirt and dilapidation, with torn window curtains, knocked-over trash cans and old rusty appliances everywhere. The apathetic look of abject poverty was on every face. In the vegetable market, we learned of a yachtie who'd been mugged an hour earlier. Even in our oldest, grubbiest clothes, and devoid of rings and watches, we constantly looked over our shoulders to make sure we weren't being followed.

It looked to be a very long month.

About two weeks into our stay, we had the chance to be line handlers on a 45-foot fiberglass sloop. The captain, Dick Allsopp, a superb seaman who kept *Mufti* in mint condition, had been making Canal transits for years. He knew every inch of the route. His heavy and well-lubricated winches provided the leverage required to manage the lines easily. In the last lock, we had powered out long before the vortex got started. With the right equipment and a little concentration, we discovered, the transit was simple.

As we moved from one lock to the next, we learned that Dick was the second in command for the U.S. Naval Fleet in Panama. With a lifelong interest in military and political history, he enthusiastically swapped war stories with Tom. He and his wife Rosemary were opera fans and had recordings of many of the operas I'd seen live at The Metropolitan Opera. Rosemary, possessed of a sardonic sense of humor, regaled us with endless tales about the frustrations of life as a military wife.

When we arrived at the Balboa Yacht Club in Panama City, where Dick moored *Mufti*, he suggested we spend the night. "Our house in Amador is only 10 minutes from downtown. We'll get you to the bus station for Colon in the morning." We accepted with enthusiasm.

Their home, a gracious white stucco bungalow with overhanging eaves designed to keep out the rain and let in the breeze, sat in the middle of an elegant residential community. With lush, green and beautifully landscaped grounds, the house was surrounded by mango trees, each more laden with fruit than the last. When we left the next morning, we carried away a shopping bag full of mangoes and a sailing invitation for the following weekend.

Clearly, there was a side to Panama we'd never been told about.

Knowing we would have to wait a month to work on *Salieri's* hull, we scheduled a trip through the San Blas Islands, a tiny archipelago 90 miles east of the Canal Zone and home to an indigenous tribe of Cuna Indians. En route to the islands, we stopped in several coastal villages that had served as major ports for the gold and spice trade between the Americas and Spain in colonial days. Now, 300 years later, we clambered over sadly overgrown stone forts. We visited imposing churches and town halls, the ancient stone crumbling beneath peeling coats of faded gold or green paint.

The San Blas, palm-dotted clumps of sand floating between the pale blue hues of sea and sky, was in better repair, but more primitive. A few pastel-painted cinderblock houses stood out vividly among the more common houses built with thatched roofs and plaited walls, laboriously constructed out of dried palm fronds. The strikingly colorful Cuna women, with straight jet-black hair and olive-skin, wore colorful but ill-matched costumes that included blouses made with traditional molas.

After 10 days of idyllic cruising, we returned to Colon and threw ourselves into the miserable task of repainting *Salieri's* hull. We hauled her out on an old-fashioned marine "railway," manually winching the boat in a rough-hewn wooden cradle out of the water on railroad tracks. It was nerve-wracking work, since we couldn't tell if we had the boat properly balanced until it was nearly out of the water. On our first attempt, the hull leaned precariously to the right and began to vibrate in the cradle. We let it back down into the water, repositioned the boat, and tried again. It was still too far to the right. Tom, typically, loved the challenge. The frustration drove me to tears.

When we finally got it right, on the third try, we began the even more gruesome task of scraping off six months of rock-hard barnacles and sanding the underwater surface until it was as smooth as a baby's skin, ready for two coats of anti-fouling paint. My back and arm muscles screamed in pain for four days. I was so ready to be gone from Panama.

It was not to be. As we slid *Salieri* back into the water, Tom noticed a small but very obvious lump just above his groin on the left side. It looked like a hernia, the occupational hazard of a desk-bound sailor. We assumed we'd have to go back to our doctor in New York, but Dick persuaded us to see his physician at the U.S. military hospital. When the doctor confirmed the diagnosis and recommended surgery, Dick assured us that the military hospital was up to U.S. standards. Dick also finagled a slip for *Salieri* at a small boatyard in the shadow of the Pedro Miguel Lock on the Pacific side of the Canal. At least we wouldn't have to spend the six weeks of Tom's convalescence in Colon.

As I looked back over the months since Florida, I had lots of good memories. Since Georgetown, we'd been part of a growing community of cruisers heading west. In every anchorage, we caught up with people we already knew and met people we'd see again.

But they were all acquaintances rather than friends. Some were young, determined to explore the world before they settled into careers and families. Others were retired couples for whom the cruise was a payoff for long years of service. Very few were like us, middle-aged, successful and willing to give it all up.

Then, too, cruising from island to island provided few

opportunities for the one-on-one conversations that I'd always used to make friends. Much as I had in New York, I let Tom take the lead in our socializing. A colorful and entertaining storyteller, he mingled easily. As we moved from one anchorage to the next, I'd listened with pleasure, relieved I didn't have to fill awkward gaps in the conversation.

Although I was rarely conscious of being lonely, by the time we reached Panama, I was hungry for the companionship of people with whom I had shared memories, people I cared about. And so, when Edith and Henry Meinninger arrived to cruise with us to the San Blas, I was thrilled. They were longtime friends and Berkshire neighbors as well as sailing companions. We'd last seen them when they cruised with us from Ft. Lauderdale to Miami.

I loved reminiscing about our walks in the Berkshire woods, our long tradition of holiday dinners, our summer picnics at Tanglewood. I wanted the latest news on Edith's consulting practice and their daughter Claudia's DNA research. I laughed as I watched Henry trying to keep his balance as he did his exercises on the bouncing foredeck each morning. But when I tried to talk about our life on *Salieri*, I couldn't seem to find the words to make it interesting.

The second evening, over cocktails, I began to describe the sights and sounds of the catboat races in Georgetown, highlighting the contrast between the aquamarine water and "the big, fluffy-white clouds." Tom interrupted. "Mary, they were cumulus clouds."

His comment startled me. Attempting to paint the backdrop for the race, I didn't need a weather report. Why did he correct such a minor detail, I wondered.

I went on. "The boats don't balance very well, because of their huge sails," I began.

"...and because they hardly have any keel." Tom interrupted again.

I ignored him. "To make the boat balance, they stick a 12-foot-long plank out on . . ."

Again, Tom. "I'm pretty sure it's longer than 12 feet."

" . . the side opposite the sail. The crew crawls as far out as they can. When the boat switches directions...."

Tom interrupted, "...when it changes tack."

"...the crew crawls back in to the cockpit, swings the plank out on the other side, and crawls back out before the sail fills. If they don't get it just right, the boat will capsize. And sometimes, if the wind lightens up with all five or six guys out on the end of the plank, the boat capsizes anyway."

Tom, one more time. "Well, they don't always have five or six guys out...it depends on the wind. Sometimes there's only two or three."

My head throbbed. It took every bit of self-control not to shout, "Shut up and let me talk." Perhaps I should have. By that point, my irritation had drowned out my initial enthusiasm, and it took conscious willpower to finish the story I'd started.

Later that evening, when we were alone, I challenged Tom. "Why did you keep interrupting me?"

"I didn't interrupt," he said with an innocent expression. "I just added a few details. After all, we were both there."

I persisted. "You did interrupt. And with details that weren't important. Why can't you let me tell my story? Why do I have to tell it your way?"

"Okay, okay." His tone was patronizing.

In fact, it happened again and again in the next few days, each time leaving me a little more off-balance. Soon, it felt easier to stop talking. To my dismay, no one seemed to notice my silence or attempted to draw me into the conversation. I felt increasingly adrift, ever more disconnected. Toward the end of their visit, I dreamt I was telling a story but no one could hear me. Once again, I felt that something was wrong, but I couldn't identify what.

By the time we returned to Panama, I knew I had to find

something to ground me. While I had no idea what it might be, that need colored my response to staying in Panama for Tom's surgery. I relished the chance to linger in one place, the opportunity to reach out for people in the leisurely way that was comfortable for me. With Tom in convalescent mode, he wouldn't be around to explain or interrupt.

Suddenly, Panama seemed the land of opportunity.

CHAPTER 8

ON AN EVEN KEEL

MY love affair with Panama began the day we moved to Pedro Miguel. As we exited the Pedro Miguel lock into a large bay, the clubhouse, a rambling, white clapboard affair with big screened windows and deep overhanging eaves, stood on our left. Half a dozen yachts in various states of disrepair lined the dock. Off to the east, near a dense jungle, I saw several unpainted metal sheds and more yachts, these sitting in land-based cradles. The club, we'd been told, was used by locals during the day but we'd have it to ourselves after 5 p.m.

The clubhouse had the comfortable feeling of old slippers. We'd expected hot showers, laundry facilities, shore power and abundant water. To my delight, we also found a well-stocked honor-system bar, a lounge with overstuffed couches, a spacious kitchen with a freezer (omigod, ice cream whenever we wanted!), a cool, airy dining room overlooking the lock and a litter of week-old kittens. A short walk through the jungle, where wild orchids grew in abundance, took us to the bus stop to downtown Panama City, less than 20 minutes away.

From the moment I stepped ashore, I felt at home. And much like East Bay Marina in Nassau, we had instant family. Russ Gudgeon, a U.S. navy lieutenant who moonlighted as the club manager, was generous with both his advice and his car. Long after we left Panama, we continued to read the history books he squirreled away for us when the library on the military base did some housecleaning.

We shared the clubhouse with Fred (also a navy lieutenant) and Cynthia. More evenings than not, we did potluck in the kitchen while we followed Iran-gate, dissected Panamanian politics, and watched the parade of ships—Japanese containerships, Russian submarines, the Queen Mary—under the blazing lights of the lock. For a time, we were joined by John and Liz, like us, midlife drop-outs en route to the rest of the world. Unlike us, they had two carrot-haired boys, one little more than a toddler, with boundless curiosity and even more boundless energy.

Dick and Rosemary came closest to being real family. We stayed with them the night of Tom's surgery and Rosemary kept in constant touch in the days immediately afterwards. In that first week, while Tom slept, she gave me guided tours of Panama City, showing me where to get the best fresh bread, where to buy free-range chicken, where to have my film developed. At first, I thought they were being kind to us but I soon I realized that we brought a different and much-appreciated perspective into their often parochial military world.

Once Tom was mobile, they took us out on *Mufti,* so he could be on the water without having to do any work. Several times a month, we sailed to Isla Taboga, a popular weekend swimming and fishing spot about two hours sail from Panama City. Typically, we anchored in deep water off the long sandy beach, swimming off the boat and eating on board. On occasion, however, we dinghied ashore and strolled along the cobbled streets until we found a restaurant or bakery that appealed to our taste at that moment.

I began to talk again.

When I told my mother about Tom's hernia, I mentioned we'd be in Panama for several months. That was a mistake.

I went immediately to find Tom when I got her letter. He lay stretched out on the cabin top under the awning, reading about Rommel in North Africa during WWII.

"You'll never guess what came in the mail today!" I held the letter by its edge between my thumb and forefinger, as if it was tainted.

"So…what is it?" He grinned, expecting something nice. He obviously missed the distress in my voice.

"My mother is arriving October 15th for a week."

"You're kidding. Why on earth would she want to come to Panama?"

"Uhhh, well, maybe she misses her son-in-law," I said with a smirk. "Who knows what moves her to do the things she does?" My shoulders slumped as I thought about her visit. "She's booked her tickets, so I guess she's coming."

"Where's she gonna stay?"

"She seems to think she's staying with us."

Tom sat bolt up. "No way! Even if she could manage to clamber on and off the boat—which she can't—I'm not going to share this small space with your mother." He paused. "Could we put her in the clubhouse?"

"No, there are no sleeping facilities there." I replied. "We'll have to get her a hotel room in town. Rosemary will know of something nice. If we rent a car while she's here, we can get back and forth easily enough."

Tom reached out and took my right hand. "Don't worry, darling, we'll get through it."

I wasn't so sure.

My earliest memories of my mother are suffused with a sense of abiding hatred. At an early age, I understood that everything I did was wrong—too late or too early, too slow or too fast, not neat enough, not clever enough, not responsible enough. By age five or six, I'd figured out that if she learned I wanted something, she'd make sure I didn't get it. Already, I knew I was expected to anticipate what she wanted without her having to tell me. As I moved into my teens, she mocked the things I liked—my school play, Elvis, wearing bobby socks or a twin set—as silly things that someone "as smart as you" shouldn't care about.

For a time, I found comfort and protection in the broad, encircling arms of my grandfather. Every day after school, he waited to greet me with his secret stash of date bread and cream cheese. But he died just before I turned seven, leaving me bereft.

My father, a bear-huggish sort of man, provided a constant source of adventure. He took me flying in a friend's private plane on Sunday mornings, to the stock car races on Saturday nights, and gave me diving lessons at the community pool. But by the time I was seven, my parents' marriage was in trouble and his attentions to me invariably sparked my mother's rage. He became increasingly unreliable as my protector.

Thereafter, I survived by staying out of my mother's line of sight. I kept my thoughts to myself. I had a huge sense of relief when I was sent off to boarding school at age 12. During high school and college, I found myriad reasons not to go home for vacations and summers.

After I got out of college, our relationship seemed to improve. My father had died and she lived alone. As I progressed through graduate school into the working world, we could generally find enough neutral topics to fill a phone call or a dinnertime discussion. With a growing network of supportive friends and a steady string of professional successes, I was no longer so vulnerable to her criticism. Even so, I consciously kept the details of my day-to-day life away from her. I made sure I could escape to my own world when her mockery became intolerable.

For a decade, we were almost companionable. An interesting and thoughtful woman, she had developed a successful career long before feminism had a name. For several years, we took a week-long vacation together—one year to Ireland, another to New England in the fall, a third to High Point and Thomasville to buy furniture for my New York apartment. After Tom and I bought the Berkshire house, she came for a week each summer. Although she and Tom got on amiably, they were not close.

Things worked well enough until the summer of 1981, the year we hired an architect to draw up plans for a new garage for the Berkshire house. It would have a guest room above, an elegant space with its own entrance, a cathedral ceiling and windows overlooking the Green River. The architect delivered the plans during her week with us. Even though we couldn't begin the work for at least a year (until the plumbing and the new kitchen were complete), we pored over the drawings with enthusiasm.

A few days after she returned home to Aiken, South Carolina, she called. "Mary, I've decided to lend you the money to do the wing now."

I noticed she didn't ask if we wanted to borrow the money. Trying to keep the cynicism out of my voice, I asked, "What prompted that?"

"Aiken's hotter than the hinges of hell during July and August. It would be nice to spend those months in the Berkshires instead of here. And having me in the wing would give you and Tom more privacy than having me in the main house."

"Hummh, interesting." It was the word I used when I

couldn't think of what else to say. And then, I added, "You mentioned 'lending' us the money. What do you have in mind?"

"Well, you pay me the interest I'd earn on Treasuries. I don't care when you pay me back."

I floated the idea by Tom that night at dinner. He echoed my concern. "I hope she isn't expecting us to treat her like a guest for two months."

"Tom, she's so active in Aiken...walks two miles every day, plays bridge and golf several times a week. She loves the arts. I can't fathom she'll sit around for the five days each week we're not here. And if she's involved in Berkshire activities during the week, she'll be involved on the weekends." I paused. "But, you're right. I need to make that point up front."

Tom leaned across the table, putting his hand on mine. "Do you really want to do this?"

I shrugged. "Absolutely not. But I know that's a reaction to things that happened 30 years ago. The last few summers have gone pretty well. Maybe we've all grown up."

Tom patted my cheek. "Mary-pie, it's your call. I know how hard it was when you were little. But if you're okay with it, it's fine with me."

I called her the next day. "We're interested. But there're two things we have to agree on."

"They are...?"

"Well, the first is that you have to make a life for yourself while you're here...find a golf foursome...join a book club... the kinds of things you do in Aiken."

She laughed amiably. "Mary, I'm surprised you feel the need to say that. I don't plan to stare at the walls when you and Tom are in the city during the week. So what's the other condition?"

"Well, it's trivial, but symbolic. We don't want to pay interest on the loan when you're living in the wing."

"So...I'll be paying rent to visit my daughter?"

I swallowed hard, feeling the knife-edge of guilt. "No. Mother, remember...you're not coming to visit your daughter. You're coming to stay in your apartment in the Berkshires."

I heard a long sigh on the other end of the phone. "Okay, okay. I get the message. I'll send you a check."

I nodded, surprised at how easily an awkward discussion had been disposed of. It made me uneasy.

I heard her voice. "Mary, are you still there?"

I realized she could not see my gesture through the phone. "We'll be happy to accept your offer."

We completed the wing by the following summer. Mother arrived the last week in June 1982. During the first few weeks, we introduced her to everyone we knew who might be of interest to her. She never followed up with anyone. She never set up a foursome for golf or bridge, she didn't join the League of Women Voters, she didn't go to concerts or movies. Instead, she devoted herself to making our weekends easy.

Her initial contribution was Friday night dinner. The second week, our phone rang on Monday night. "Hi, Mary-pie. How's your week?"

My week had barely begun and I didn't have much to say. Then too, her use of my pet name rankled. In fact, she had given me the nickname when I was a child and Tom had picked it up from her years earlier. Irrationally, I now felt it belonged to Tom, and saw it as an unwarranted familiarity when she used it. My reply was terse. "Okay. What's up?"

"How about scallops for dinner Friday?"

"Mother, I don't know what our plans are. We may not get there until late." My jaw felt tight. I knew what was coming.

"But you and Tom have to eat. I'll have scallops ready when you get here."

"Mother," I tried to sound firm. "Please...I don't want you to make dinner for us."

"No, really, I'm delighted to do it. I'll see you about eight unless you tell me differently."

I let my annoyance come through. "Mother, do not plan dinner for us on Friday. We may decide to meet friends. Or if we get a late start, we may stop for pizza on the way."

"Mary, don't be silly. Why would you want pizza when you could have fresh scallops? I'll have dinner ready unless I hear differently by tomorrow." She hung up before I could say any more.

I called her Wednesday to tell her we'd been invited to friends for dinner.

"Mary, I've ordered the scallops already."

"Mother, I told you last night not to plan on us Friday night."

"I was just trying to be helpful," she whined. "If you don't want me to do anything for you, I'll stay out of your way. I'll eat alone on Friday night. Don't worry about me."

I knew it would be a long summer.

I took that first summer—only 12 days spread over six weeks—in my stride. And each time I talked about her making a life for herself in the Berkshires, she regaled me with information she'd gathered on things to do the following summer "once I'm really settled in."

In fact, the second summer was worse than the first. Increasingly, we felt we were the visitors in her house. She served lunch at 12:30 on Saturdays and Sundays, whether or not we were hungry, whether or not we had plans with friends, whether or not we were in the middle of a task that could not be put down. When we went out to do errands or meet friends for a concert, she insisted on knowing when we would return and got decidedly grumpy if we returned later than we'd said.

She insisted on doing the dishes, all the dishes. If Tom and I lingered over conversation—as we were wont to do in the country—she got up and began to hover once she had finished her food.

"Tom, can I take that plate for you?" she'd ask as soon as he put down his fork.

"No, I'll put it in the dishwasher when we're done."

"I'm happy to clean up. You and Mary work so hard during the week. You don't need the extra burden of dishes."

"Kathryn, I may have a second helping. Don't take the plate just yet."

"What would you like…more meat…more salad? I'll get it for you."

"I'm not sure I want more. I just want to sit for a bit and then decide."

"Alright. If you don't want my help, that's fine. I'll just go to my room."

Where she'd mocked the things I wanted as a child, now she simply pretended they didn't exist. She managed to forget that I had a standing tennis game on Saturday and Sunday mornings and invariably greeted me on Friday night with a project for us to do together on Saturday. She whined if I made lunch plans with friends when "I've come all the way from Aiken to spend time with my daughter." Frequently, she moaned that I didn't appreciate her. More often, she retreated to her room in a huff. When all else failed, she reminded me that "It was my money that paid for the wing in your house."

During that second summer, I reminded her repeatedly about finding connections in the Berkshires. Her standard response was "I do lots of things when you're not here during the week." Curiously, she never shared any details of what those things were.

When I reminded her, in a phone conversation before the third summer, she laughed. "Mary, there are a lot of things I want to do while I'm in the Berkshires." But when the summer came, still she did not look for a golf foursome or a bridge game or a friend for the movies. To this day, I don't know whether she was willfully lying to me or just kidding herself.

And then, in that third summer, I realized with horror just how much I was like her. My blood ran cold when I saw how often I did to Tom the things I most hated when she did them to me…how often I expected him to know what I wanted without my having to tell him…how often I took offense when he simply wanted something different than I did.

Watching her made me twice angry, once for how she treated me and once for having been so inadequate a role model. I felt trapped by her—and trapped by my inability to not be like her. As much as I loved my garden and my Saturday tennis game, I began to find reasons to stay in the city on the weekends when she was in residence. When I did go to the country, she and I fought constantly.

By the end of the summer of 1984, Tom and I agreed to pay off the loan and tell her she couldn't come for more than a week. I dreaded that conversation. I put it off for months. And then, in January 1985, we decided to go sailing. I didn't go sailing to avoid my mother, but it certainly solved a problem I didn't want to deal with.

The sailing trip broke the pattern. We didn't have a schedule, so she couldn't plan a visit. We didn't have a phone, so she couldn't call. As we made our way down the East Coast, my calls to her became increasingly less frequent. Once we left for the Bahamas, our communications were almost entirely by letter. I liked it that way.

I didn't want her to come to Panama. I didn't want her to critique the decorating scheme—or lack thereof—of the club-house, which we loved. I didn't want her to tell me that my haircut—low maintenance for a life with limited water—didn't flatter my face. I didn't want her to complain that my clothes—mostly drip dry for life without an electric drier—looked scruffy. And given the effort Tom and I had put into learning to live as a team on *Salieri*, I didn't want to look at her and see the reflection of all the things I had not yet managed to get right.

Once Tom was out of pain, he chafed under Mosquera's orders not to drive, hike or do any boat work. Desperate for something to do besides read, he offered to set up a computerized bookkeeping system for the club at Pedro Miguel. Russ declined his offer but referred him to a Canadian friend who owned a business selling a curious mix of high-tech electronics and low-tech steel cable to the Japanese and Central American tuna fleets that worked the Eastern Pacific.

With Rosemary as my tour guide, my days were full. Even so, the idea of working in Panama appealed to me. So, Tom and I put on our best jeans and called on Mel. To our astonishment, he offered us both jobs on the spot, a half-time job for Tom to evaluate a proposed business acquisition, a half-time job for me to install an automated inventory system. We were to come back the next day to negotiate final details, after he'd made the necessary arrangements for our work visas.

We were all but dancing as we headed back to the bus station. Tom's voice bubbled. "This is gonna be fun."

My face hurt from grinning so hard. "Wow, it never dawned on me that we'd find work so quickly—or that getting a work visa would be so easy. A few paces on, I said, "Mel didn't talk about money. What do you think he'll pay us?"

"I'm going to ask for $100 a day."

"How'd you figure that?"

"Well, a good wage in Panama is $10 a day and most people make only $5–6, so $100 seems pretty aggressive. He probably won't agree to it, but it's a place to start."

"I wonder what a professional makes in Panama. Maybe we could get more."

"I doubt it. I'm going to go for $100."

The next morning, Mel agreed to $100 so quickly I knew we could have gotten more. Somehow, it didn't matter. With a cruising budget of $150 a week, $100 a day made us rich.

Working changed our perspective on Panama yet again. First of all, it forced us to learn the language. Mel's Panamanian staff was bilingual and happy to help when we couldn't find the right word. Within a few weeks, we could navigate through social occasions as well as work.

Living and working in Panama also forced us to confront cultural norms we never would have noticed as cruisers. We adapted readily to siesta, the only antidote to the immobilizing midday heat. Working until 8 p.m. was also easy enough, after years of long hours in New York. But our Protestant work ethic rebelled at the concept of manãna. The dictionary says it means "tomorrow." Our first day on the job, however, we learned that it means "not now"…"go away"…"I don't want to discuss it." The New Yorker in me grew wildly frustrated, annoyed beyond measure at being put off, at people's unwillingness to confront issues or make decisions.

Problematic in a different way was the practice of a leisurely, well-lubricated dinner starting at 10 p.m. and ending as we fell into bed at midnight or 1 a.m. Neither my stomach nor my head ever adjusted. And it was a constant struggle. Because we were making plenty of money by local standards, we were soon included in the social life of Panama City.

Through Mel and his sublimely sexy Panamanian wife Marta, we were introduced to the world of private clubs, art gallery openings and weekend house parties. We hosted picnics with checkered tablecloths and fresh flowers, and were invited to backyard barbecues with goat and chorizo instead of hamburgers and hot dogs. We dined at elegant waterfront restaurants and gave dinner parties in the Pedro Miguel clubhouse. We went to the ballet, the symphony and the movies.

In many ways, the world of the Panamanian middle and upper classes looked much like the world we'd known in New York. One notable exception was the "push-button" motel, a local institution designed for a small city where most everyone lived at home and everyone knew everyone else. Having located an open garage door, a couple seeking privacy could, by pushing a button, close the garage door and gain access to a private suite with, depending on the price level, a range of sex toys, blue movies and dining options without ever coming face to face with anyone.

Less familiar was the world of the Canal Zone, the clubby, inbred world of the military on overseas duty, which we saw at close range through Dick and Rosemary. Dick knew everyone in Panama, including Manuel Noriega, at that time a staunch ally of the Americans. Dick also knew all the members of the Arias family, Panama's equivalent of the Rockefellers; what he could accomplish with a phone call made the New York business world seem child's play. Somewhat shocking to me, he seemed oblivious to the adult men who visibly groveled in response to his smallest wish. Even more shocking, Dick visibly groveled at the Admiral's smallest wish. I was at once fascinated and repelled. But Dick's love of sailing, opera and history, and Rosemary's unfailing ability to make us laugh, made them delightful company. We spent many weekends on *Mufti,* often taking overnight trips to Taboga, a small, sun-bleached island about two hours west of Panama City.

As the weeks passed, Tom and I fell back into the mode of parallel lives that had characterized our life in New York and to a lesser extent in Marathon. I loved the challenge of trying to motivate staff resistant to new ways of doing things. Tom was absorbed in evaluating Mel's business target. We shared the routine household tasks on the basis of who got there first, just as we'd done in New York. I still let Tom take the lead at gatherings with strangers, but once I started working, I had my own stories to tell. My concern about disappearing faded away.

One Saturday afternoon in late September, about a month after Tom's surgery, we stopped for lunch at La Estancia, a tiny outdoor bistro that served only grilled chicken, fresh green salad and a crisp Argentinean wine.

Holding up his glass of gently chilled white, Tom offered a toast. "To our favorite lunch spot." He tilted his chair back to balance on the two rear legs and stretched out his arms, his hands resting on the back of his head. "Did you ever think we'd have a favorite lunch spot in Panama?"

I grinned. "Nope. In those first weeks, I couldn't imagine liking anything about Panama."

He brought his chair back to the floor. "You know, I see Mosquera tomorrow. If he gives me a clean bill of health, we could leave anytime."

His comment startled me. We still had a lot to do for Mel. My mother would be arriving mid-October. An image of picking fresh orchids for the dinner table as I walked from the bus stop through the jungle each evening flashed through my mind. "Tom, I don't want to leave. At least not anytime soon."

He sat for a moment, swirling the wine around the bowl of his glass. "I don't know what I want to do. I like working with Mel. And Panama's certainly interesting. But I miss sailing." He paused, "How much longer do you want to stay?"

I shook my head. "I don't know…until it's no longer interesting, I guess." I remembered that day in Belhaven, when Alan, the harbormaster, advised us to let things just happen rather than plan too carefully. We'd long since given up any hope of adhering to the original itinerary, but a decision to stay in Panama implied an entirely different sort of adventure than we had in mind the day we left New York.

Tom gave me a long look. "I'm okay with that. But if we want to avoid the cyclone season in the Western Pacific, we'll need to leave by February."

As a surge of adrenaline shot through me, I blew him a kiss. "Tom, that's practically a lifetime." I wondered if this was another of those life-changing, spur-of-the-moment decisions.

When Tom went for his hernia checkup, his doctor removed a small black mole from his upper back, just over his spine. The biopsy showed a malignant melanoma. A one-inch wide swath of the upper three layers of Tom's back would have to be removed. The doctor scheduled Tom for outpatient surgery the next afternoon. For the first time, I saw fear in Tom's eyes.

We were both in shock. Fortunately, Dick and Rosemary took charge, making whatever arrangements were needed. Knowing that Tom would be immobilized for a week or more, they insisted we move into their home until Tom could get on and off the boat easily. The next morning Rosemary drove us to the hospital and came back to pick us up when Tom came out of recovery. By 7:30 that night, Tom sat munching a roast beef sandwich in Allsopps' kitchen and discussing the North African invasion during WWII with Dick.

I couldn't see much point in talking about our options until we had the results of the biopsy. And so, Tom caught me off-guard next morning, as we sat at the kitchen table over a leisurely breakfast. Dick had left for work hours earlier. Rosemary was at a charity function.

Laying the paper down on the table, Tom took my hand. "I'm not going back to the States. I don't care what the biopsy says."

Hearing a tremor in his voice, I wondered whether he was trying to convince me or himself. "What if you need chemo?"

He shook his head. "I'll do it in Panama." He paused, his fingers moving slowly across my hand. When he spoke again, his tone was almost fierce. "Mary, so many of my family have died of cancer. If the tumor has spread, I'm not going home and wait for it to get me. I want to finish this trip."

For a brief moment, I was hurt that he didn't ask what I thought he should do or how I felt about his decision. But I understood. In my early 20s, I'd watched helplessly as my father suffered through the complications of diabetes. Although we all knew he'd never get better, my mother acceded to the stronger will of his doctor, a physician who insisted on one surgery after another, on reviving him each time his heart failed. A decade later, Tom and I had watched, equally helplessly, as his father struggled with the side-effects of chemotherapy that did nothing to arrest his lung cancer. I knew Tom—a man who was determined to push the envelope, to test the limits—would not give up a minute of life if he didn't have to.

When the pathology report came—a report later confirmed by Sloan Kettering Cancer Center in New York—we were exuberant. Tom read it to me over lunch in *Salieri*'s cockpit. "The tumor," he read, "is self-contained and slow-growing. Based on the biopsy sample, the mass has been completely removed. There are no indications that radiation or chemotherapy is required."

Over the next week, I read the report several times a day, just to reassure myself Tom really was okay.

During the next two months, we explored Panama by boat and by car. The high point proved to be a weeklong trip into the mountains in the north, where we visited an elderly Catholic priest, Father Phillip whom Tom had met on the ham radio net. His small mud-brick house, perched on the side of a mountain, was simply furnished and without central heat. Despite the tropical latitude, we needed several layers of wool clothes during the day. At night, we were grateful for his thick down comforters.

Father Phillip was intrigued by our plan to cross the Pacific Ocean, particularly when he found we planned to visit Tonga. He spoke excitedly of a missionary there, a friend from seminary days. "Would you," he asked, "take a package to him from me?" We pulled out an atlas and found Tonga. Our route would take us past the Ha'apai Islands where Brother Chris ran the Catholic school. Tom, ever the adventurer, agreed.

And, of course, my mother arrived, three weeks after Tom's second surgery. There was no way we could put her up at Pedro

Miguel, so we arranged for an elegant residential hotel in Panama City, less than 20 minutes away. Since Russ and Dick were generous enough to lend us cars throughout the week, we were able to go back and forth with ease and on short notice. Much to our relief, she described the hotel as "very comfortable."

By the time she arrived, Tom was mobile but not very, so we filled several days touring Panama City and its environs by car. Two or three days, Mother and I spent together on our own, sampling the lunch fare at one or another of Panama City's charming eateries, including La Estancia, the little Argentine bistro where Tom and I had made another of our fateful decisions. When we decided to visit local art galleries and explore the open-air markets, Rosemary served as our tour guide. From her comments, I gathered that Mother liked the food and was impressed with a number of the local artists, but found the markets too chaotic for her taste.

Our evenings were full as well. One night, Rosemary and Dick invited us to their home for dinner; another they took us out for paella at a tiny bistro looking out over the Pacific Ocean. Several evenings, Tom and I took her to one of the elegant waterfront restaurants in Panama City.

On Tom's birthday, we spent the day at Pedro Miguel cooking. We'd planned a dinner party for 12 in the clubhouse, where we could watch the nighttime traffic under the blazing lights of the canal. Mother whined briefly when she learned we wanted her to make a cherry cheesecake pie—her specialty—without the aid of an electric mixer, but she got into the spirit of things and the pie was delicious.

Throughout the week, she was amiable and gracious, an entertaining and lively woman I'd all too rarely seen. As we put her on the plane home, I could honestly tell her I was glad she'd come.

And then, two weeks later, I got her "thank you" note. In it, she vented her rage at our having "stashed" her in a hotel when she wanted to stay with us at Pedro Miguel. She complained that the schedule of lunches and dinners had been "forced" on her, with no concern for what might interest her. She was dismayed at "never being allowed" to experience the rhythm of our daily life. It was, she said in closing, "one of the worst vacations I've ever had."

I was stunned. We'd introduced her to our friends. We'd taken her to all the places that were significant in our world. She'd shared with us the challenge of making a party in a foreign land. What had I missed? Could she have been pretending when she praised the food, the hotel, our friends, the local artists? Had she made complaints that I somehow hadn't heard?

Reading her letter through the second time, I realized I didn't care. In Panama, for the first time, her rage washed over me without effect. I was genuinely sorry she hadn't enjoyed the trip. But she'd invited herself without bothering to find out what the conditions of her visit would be. I had no interest in postmortems, no interest in apologizing or trying to make reparations.

I never responded to that letter. The next time I wrote to her, I pretended I hadn't received it. I told her how much we'd enjoyed her visit. I told her that we hoped she'd visit us again along the way, knowing, as I wrote it, that I would never again give her enough information on our sailing schedule to allow her to visit.

The appeal of Panama was rediscovering who I'd been when I was in New York...or perhaps reinventing myself as the person I wanted to be when I left New York to see the world. Panama was everything I hoped it would be. I loved the challenge of installing Mel's inventory system. I enjoyed the comfortable, reassuring routine with Rosemary and Cynthia. And most of all, I was happy that Tom and I had reconnected, that we found lots to talk about, that we enjoyed exploring the countryside together. All seemed right with my world.

And yet ... it bothered me that Tom and I had re-created, in so many ways, the frenetic lifestyle we had in New York. I broached the subject over dinner in November, one of the few evenings when we were eating alone.

"Tom, isn't it curious," I asked, "that, in a country that's by nature indolent, where manãna rules, we have more things to do than time to do them?"

Tom smiled, knowingly. "Don't you remember how, when we were planning the trip, we wondered if we'd be satisfied with a life that had no purpose, how we'd cope with having nothing we had to do? I think the answer is clearly no."

I nodded in agreement. "I know the feeling. I need something to do that exercises my brain, that gives me a purpose." I reached over, took his right hand and kissed it. "I get a little scared thinking about cruising again, months on end without friends, without a project to occupy me. What if I start to disappear again?"

"Maybe we should change our itinerary a bit." Tom leaned forward, his elbows on the table, his chin on his fists. "Why does this trip have to be only five years? What if we stop along the way...stay in countries where we can work?"

I felt a rush of adrenaline. "Where do you s'pose the next place is that we could work?"

Tom looked into the middle distance. I could see him mentally tracing the map across the Pacific. "Maybe Tahiti. Certainly New Zealand."

"Count me in," I said with gusto. *Another spur-of-the moment, life-changing decision.*

By mid-December, I was beginning to do things out of habit rather than out of curiosity. Our learning curve had leveled off. As the projects for Mel were nearly done, we began to make plans for our departure.

I spent many hours wandering through the local produce

markets in search of fresh foods that would last on a boat. It was critical to buy things that had never been refrigerated. Off the back of a small truck, I bought nearly a bushel of green tomatoes, which I wrapped in newspaper and stored in the bilge; as long as the tomatoes remained cool and dry, they would ripen only when I unwrapped them. From a heavyset farm wife hovering over huge piles of vegetables, I bought a dozen large cabbages, knowing that the core of a cabbage will stay crisp as long as it is peeled rather than cut. In a nearby stall, I picked up dozens of onions, lemons, limes, grapefruits and oranges, all of which came in naturally preserved packaging. Regretfully, I passed up carrots and beans; both go soggy with salt air almost immediately.

There were other tricks as well. I managed to find unrefrigerated eggs which, if wiped with Vaseline and turned periodically, last indefinitely. I looked for mayonnaise and mustard in squeeze bottles that would not need to be refrigerated, since they would not get contaminated by other foods. I purchased a large container of unpasteurized yogurt so I would have a culture to make my own yogurt during the months on the Pacific. I bought several pounds of alfalfa seeds to grow sprouts.

Tom, of course, focused on the mechanical stuff. He sold our small dinghy and 2HP engine to some locals and bought (duty-free, even!) a six-person dinghy and a 25-HP engine that would get us through almost any sea condition. Although *Salieri's* tanks held 100 gallons each of water and fuel, he acquired a dozen five-gallon jugs, red to match our sail covers. He filled six with water and six with diesel fuel, and lashed them all on the forward deck.

We enjoyed the provisioning process in Panama, in part because we were more confident about what we needed to do than we had been the first time in Marathon. But much of the pleasure came from realizing how easily we were able to find our way around a foreign land, how much we had learned about living in this unique and colorful country.

As we provisioned, we found ourselves constantly negotiating over quantity and price, a process that offered an insight into how much we had changed since leaving New York. Bargaining was a social pastime, a discovery process in which the final price was less important than playing the game well. I did it easily in the open-air markets, since I was familiar with market prices and negotiations rarely involved more than a few pennies. But I watched with pride as Tom haggled over the cost of the new outboard engine and managed to save several hundred dollars.

A year earlier, he couldn't have pulled it off. In fact, the first few times we tried to bargain we embarrassed ourselves and the merchant involved. Having grown up in a world where no one ever bargained—my mother had told me repeatedly that "if you have to ask the price, you can't afford it"—we didn't handle it well. We got annoyed if our efforts to negotiate failed and felt guilty when they succeeded.

The turning point came in a produce market in the Dominican Republic, where I routinely bought mangos. For several weeks, my mango lady had demanded 25 centavos per mango. I had forced myself to bargain, whittling her down to 20 centavos each (about 5 cents compared to $2 in New York). Her somber face, as she handed over my mangos, exacerbated my feeling of guilt.

On that legendary day, with my much-improved Spanish, I stood in line as a local housewife negotiated a dozen mangoes for 20 centavos, a bit more than a penny apiece! With my newfound knowledge, I asked for a dozen for 20 when my turn came. She shook her head firmly and offered five. We finally settled on eight for 20 centavos, not as good as the local housewife got, but much less than I had been paying.

But the real lesson came when my mango lady winked at me as she gave me my bag of fruit. In that instant, I understood that, even as I had tried to rationalize my guilt, my fruit lady viewed me as an ignorant *tourista*, an easy target. Now that I knew how to play the game, I had joined the ranks of her regular customers.

As our departure date drew closer, I had the odd moment of anxiety about trying to cope for months at a time without the stimulation of work and friends. But Tom and I had overcome so many obstacles. We had learned a lot about ourselves and our relationship. I had grown comfortable with life on a sailboat. I looked forward to studying Darwin and evolution in the Galapagos, to exploring the land of Melville and Jack London in the Central Pacific. The prospect of working and living in other countries thrilled me. I could hardly wait to leave.

The best—and the worst—were yet to come.

CHAPTER 9

SAILING AT THE
EDGE—AGAIN

DICK loped across the club's broad, scruffy expanse of lawn, Rosemary trailing behind. Along with Eric and Marina McVittie, they'd agreed to be line handlers on our last trip through the two locks between Pedro Miguel and the Pacific Ocean.

Tom, on the dock coiling up our heavy yellow power cable around his elbow, called out to them, "All aboard. Next stop, San Cristobal in the Galapagos!"

Halting in mid-step, Dick held up his hands in mock resistance. "Whoa, Captain. I hope you're planning a brief stop at Balboa before you head out to sea."

Tom laughed, "I'll give it serious thought…but no guarantees! I may just take you folks along as ballast."

We were in high spirits. Each of the places we planned to visit—the Galapagos, Tahiti, Tonga—would offer a unique cultural perspective. The prospect of working in Tahiti or New Zealand was exciting.

By the time the Canal pilot arrived for our 9 a.m. start, everything was stowed and we were eager to get started. The transit through Miraflores Lock #1 was uneventful. As we waited for the lock gates to open to the Pacific Ocean after the water dropped in Miraflores #2, however, I noticed that the digital gauge on the sonar was blank.

"Tom, the depth sounder isn't getting a reading."

"It was okay a few minutes ago," he said distractedly, intent on getting us out of the lock as soon as possible after the gates opened. "We're probably sitting on an oil slick. It'll be fine once we're underway."

That had happened to us before, and I didn't have time to think about it anyway. When the gates opened, we had to work fast to pull in the lines released by the Canal staff on the walls 50 feet above us. We got *Salieri* out of the lock in less than 30 seconds. As we cleared the lock, I remembered how scary that maneuver had been on *Mini Boat*.

It was only a few minutes from there to the dock in Balboa. After topping up our diesel tanks, we broke out a bottle of champagne, along with paté and cheese. For several hours, we reminisced about the good times we'd shared in the past seven months. Midafternoon, the Allsopps and the McVitties clambered off *Salieri* amid several rounds of hugs and buckets of tears.

Tom and I set sail for Taboga. We arrived at sunset, the golden red rays backlighting the tile-roofed bungalows that run the length of the island. Early the next morning, while the air was still cool, we went ashore for a last visit to the island where we'd spent so many pleasant days. We strolled leisurely along the cobbled streets of the village, engraving into our memories the pastel houses framed by bougainvillea in fuschia, flaming coral and dazzling white. When we got to the "panaderia," we claimed an outdoor table and ordered rich dark espresso and several of the fruit-laden pastries we'd come to love. We lolled there for more than an hour, a bit reluctant to make the final break.

By noon, we'd lashed the dinghy on the foredeck and were ready for the 10-day passage to the Galapagos. Tom switched on the SatNav and the instrument panel and went on deck to get the sails ready. I stowed lunch dishes, battened down the last few loose items, and pulled out the chart for the seas just west of Panama.

A few minutes later, Tom came below, his brow furrowed. "It's weird," he said. "We're still not getting a reading on the depth sounder."

I pointed to the SatNav screen, mounted on the wall just opposite the galley. "Umm, we haven't had a position fix since midnight, either."

Tom groaned as he played with the SatNav buttons. "This close to the equator, we shouldn't go more than three or four hours without a fix."

I could feel a knot in my stomach. "Tom, let's call Mel. He's the electronics guru. Let's see what he thinks we should do."

"Nah…we don't need to bother Mel. I'm sure it's just a coincidence. I can't believe they both broke."

I had a nagging memory of problems we created for ourselves in the ICW without reverse gear. But this time, we'd be out on the Pacific Ocean, with no coast guard to come to our rescue if something went wrong.

"Tom, humor me. Call Mel."

"Mary, you worry too much. We'll be just fine."

My skin prickled. That's what he'd said just before we hit the sandbar in Florida. In the space of a few seconds, it seemed we'd rolled the clock back nearly a year.

I thought about picking up the VHF and calling Mel. But I didn't. Why? Perhaps because the skies were clear, the seas were flat, and the southeast wind, 10–12 knots, was perfect for our course to the Galapagos. Perhaps because I didn't want to have a fight with Tom before we'd started our first day's sail. Perhaps because I wanted the SatNav and depth sounder to be okay. Whatever the reason, I helped Tom raise the sails and we headed out.

Tom had the first watch. I went below to read, but fell asleep to *Salieri's* cradling motion. When I awoke for my watch at 4 p.m., the wind was up to 20 knots. It had also clocked around from the east and now blew from directly behind us. We were sailing "dead down," with the mainsail swung all the way out to starboard.

My pulse started to race. With the seas rolling up under our stern, *Salieri* skidded down the face of the larger waves. Each time we slid off a wave, the apparent wind—the direction of the wind as it crossed *Salieri's* deck—shifted, sometimes sneaking over to the starboard side of the center line. Each time the wind crossed that line, the mainsail lost the wind that kept it full and the boom swung in toward the center of the boat. Sailing dead down in this sea was risky. If the apparent wind shifted enough, we'd jibe, causing the 16-foot long, solid maple boom to swing all the way over to the other side of the boat. With 20 knots of wind, a jibe could damage the mast or the supporting stays.

I noticed that Tom had mounted a boomvang, a complex arrangement of lines and tackle running from the deck to the middle of the boom. The vang was designed to hold the boom in place with fluky winds. It wasn't designed to hold the boom in place if 20 knots of wind got on the wrong side of the mainsail.

I perched on the top step of the companionway where I could watch the sails and talk to Tom, at the saloon table writing up the logbook. "Did you ever get a reading on the depth sounder? Or a SatNav fix?" I asked.

"No, but we were off soundings within a mile of Taboga.

And I'm pretty sure the SatNav problem is the aerial. I can fix that easily enough. We're fine"

"But we don't really know, do we?" I frowned. "Tom, I want to turn back. The nearest place to fix electronic gear is Tahiti. That's 5,000 miles away. There are a lot of low-lying islands and unpredictable currents between here and there."

"Mary, you're being ridiculous. The odds they both broke in a 24-hour period are minimal. I'll tell you what...if we don't have a SatNav fix by tomorrow morning, we'll go back."

When I heard him say 'ridiculous,' the knot in my stomach ground tighter. We'd had this same discussion a year earlier and the result nearly ended the trip.

"Okay, we'll revisit this tomorrow," I said reluctantly. "But right now I'm going to adjust our course. We're on the edge of a jibe."

He sounded irritated. "Mary, leave the course alone. If I thought it was risky, I wouldn't do it."

I looked at him with amazement. How could he possibly say there was no risk? He was the one who'd put the vang on. From the corner of my eye, I saw the boom jerk inboard, straining against the vang.

I stood up in the companionway. In a voice that left no room for negotiation, I said, "Tom, it's my watch and I think the odds of jibing are too high. Please come up and release the vang while I adjust the course to get us just a bit off dead down."

Tom, his pen poised over the logbook, made no move to get up. With that same note of irritation, he said, "Mary, I want to take advantage of this heading as long as we can."

I felt a wave of heat along the back of my neck. "Goddammit, it's my watch. I'm not going to spend the next four hours worrying. We're on a 10-day trip and it won't kill us to sail a few degrees off course for a few hours." The boom jerked toward the center.

"Mary, for God's sake, don't be such a worrywart."

A flash of white light shot across the back of my eyes. When I spoke again, my voice was trembling. "Tom, If you won't help me, I'll do it mys…"

I watched with horror as the boom broke, like a match stick, right where the vang was attached. The aft end of the boom swung over toward the port side and then back beyond the point where it had started, too quickly for me to fully comprehend what I was seeing.

Aloud, but not quite consciously, I said, deadpan, ". . . never mind. It doesn't matter any more." I stared as the boom jerked to port again. I was rooted to the spot.

With the noise of the wind and seas, Tom had not heard the boom break, but he felt the sudden change in *Salieri's* motion. He stood up abruptly, "Mary, what happened?"

I was in shock. More to myself than to him, I said, "The boom just broke."

Tom looked worried. "Be serious, Mary. Did we hit something? What's going on up there?

I couldn't move, couldn't think. I stared at him. "See for yourself."

Tom pushed by me to get up to the cockpit. Still standing numbly on the stairway, I flashed back to our grounding on the sandbar. At worst that day, *Salieri's* hull would have cracked, but the boat would not have sunk. Tom and I could have walked to shore in the shallow water.

Slowly, my mind returned to the present. We were in real danger. Given our erratic motion, the sail would eventually tear. If that happened, the boom could fly in almost any direction…into the sea, or into one of our skulls. If the mast fell and damaged the hull, the boat would sink. We were 50 miles off the coast of Panama. The water was several hundred feet deep. We had a life raft, but it could be days before someone came to our rescue.

I heard Tom turn on the engine. "Mary, we have to get the mainsail down." He grabbed our harnesses from the cockpit locker. He clipped his to the harness cable running along the deck so he could go forward to the mast.

I clipped mine to the steering column. "I'll turn us into the wind."

As we turned, the arc of the boom's swing steadily diminished, reducing the risk it would hit one of the stays, reducing the risk the sail would tear. But with the broken boom and heavy seas, it was hard to keep the bow steady.

"Mary, keep the bow straight into the wind," Tom called out.

"I'm trying, but it's squirrelly."

As Tom lowered the sail, the wind caught it. Several hundred square feet of heavy canvas fell into the water, the broken end of boom hanging over the right side of the boat. The resulting drag exacerbated the slewing motion as we slid down each wave.

Tom moved instinctively to the foredeck, at the forward edge of the sail, and braced himself against the lifelines. To get more stability on the bouncing deck, he attached a second harness clip to a deck cleat. I stayed near the cockpit, at the back end of the sail. I clipped my harness to the deck cable and a cleat.

We hauled the sail up, one handful of stiff, waterlogged canvas at a time. Within minutes, we were soaking wet and shivering, but we couldn't take time to go below and put on wet gear. Despite our best efforts, we could never get more than a few feet up at once. Each time the boat rolled, the wind took back much of what we'd managed to retrieve. The only way to keep the wind from stealing away what we pulled on board was to stand on it. Our footing, in the rolling seas with the slippery sail, was far from stable. We fell repeatedly. Only later did I notice the black-and-blue marks where I'd hit the gunnels, the cuts and scrapes where I'd fallen on a deck fitting.

Once the sail was lashed down on deck, we hauled in the boom, a Herculean task. Leaning out over the lifelines while the boat continued to roll, we needed brute force to pull it up on deck. Without harnesses firmly attached to the deck, one or both of us would surely have gone overboard.

By 6 p.m.—only a few minutes before dark—we'd bagged the mainsail, lashed the broken end of the boom to the deck, and set *Salieri* on a course back to Taboga. But now we were heading directly into the wind. Steep waves broke over our bow, flooding the length of the deck and the cockpit.

Where it had taken us four reasonably pleasant hours to get away from Taboga, it took us more than eight hours of pounding into the breaking waves to get back. Without sails, the windvane was useless. We had to steer manually. In the heavy seas, holding the boat on course was physically exhausting. My arms hurt. My head hurt. My eyes hurt. My shoulders hurt. I had a knot in my stomach. Tom and I spelled each other every hour. I tried to sleep when I wasn't at the helm, but with the bow slamming into the sea, that was impossible.

By the time we got to Taboga and had the anchor down, it was after 2 a.m. We turned off the engine, turned on the anchor light and fell into bed. I was asleep the instant I put my head on the pillow.

Our plight did not look much better after a night's sleep, despite the clear skies and calm seas. I couldn't begin to put into words the complex mix of anger and disappointment I felt.

As Tom steered us back toward Balboa, we discussed our options. There weren't many.

Huddled in the corner of the cockpit, I asked, "Do you think we can get a new boom in Panama?"

Tom laughed bitterly. "Not a hope in hell. No one in Panama knows how to make a wooden boom...even if they could get the right wood. It'll have to be done by a marine yard in New England."

I sighed, "That's gonna cost us, big time. Along with the SatNav and the depth sounder." Having a new boom made would take months and would almost certainly wipe out most of the funds meant to support us for the next three years. Once again, our dream cruise seemed to have come to an untimely end.

A little later, Tom turned the helm over to me. "I'm gonna call Dick and Russ. Maybe Dick can get us a temporary mooring at the yacht club in Balboa. We could go back to Pedro Miguel but I'd rather not have to go through the Canal again."

Both men were very sympathetic—and polite enough not to make jokes about our sailing skills. Dick assured us he could get a guest mooring in Balboa and agreed to meet us at the club. He also insisted that we stay at their home until we decided what to do next. I wanted to reach through the VHF radio to kiss him.

As we approached Balboa, Russ called back. "Tom, you won't believe this, but I've found you a wooden boom. It's a few inches longer than yours, but it'll work. All you have to do is reset the fittings from *Salieri*."

Tom's shouted into the mike with glee. "Russ, you're a miracle worker. How in hell did you find a wooden boom in Panama, let alone one that fits *Salieri*?"

Russ was matter-of-fact. "It's all in who you know. A friend who's a salvage operator took the mast and boom off a yacht that went up on the rocks off the west coast of Panama a month ago. They're in his warehouse. There's not much of a market for wooden booms in Panama, so I suspect you can get it for a very reasonable price."

God continues to smile on fools, I thought to myself.

Repairing *Salieri* was a surprisingly easy task. Tom set up a workshop in Allsopps' driveway and borrowed tools from Russ. Once the replacement boom was in the driveway, we sanded it down and put on several coats of varnish. The last step was transferring the chrome and brass fittings from the old boom to the new one. In the meantime, Mel's staff repaired the depth sounder and the SatNav—at awesomely discounted rates. Three weeks later, *Salieri* was ready to go.

Repairing the damage to the crew was more difficult. For days, I was so angry at Tom it was almost impossible for me to carry on a civil conversation. But as we sanded and varnished, and re-sanded and re-varnished, we began to talk.

From Tom: "I'm not sure what happened to me out there. I was so glad to be on the move again, I refused to admit that the SatNav or depth sounder might be broken. The surge of power as Salieri flew down the waves felt so good. I didn't want to miss a minute of it. But it made me take a stupid risk."

From me: "It's my fault too. I could have called Mel. I could have changed our heading. If I'd acted, instead of talking, instead of automatically deferring to you, it wouldn't have happened."

From Tom: "I have to sail more cautiously. If you'll agree to keep going, I promise I'll be more careful."

From me: "I have to learn to take more responsibility for what happens, to not sit back and let you make all the decisions."

For a while, the conversation seemed academic to me… an anatomy of an accident, but not relevant to my future. Somewhere around the third coat of varnish, I realized that Tom had, for the first time, actually acknowledged that he was at fault, that he *needed* to do things differently. He wasn't just trying to placate me.

And so, I decided—we decided—to continue on, to give this team effort another try. When the repairs on *Salieri* were done and the driveway cleaned up, we propped a thank-you note and a huge bouquet of tropical flowers on the Allsopps' kitchen counter, called a cab and left for Balboa.

At last, we were on our way.

PART III

FAIR WINDS

CHAPTER 10

THE ONE THAT GOT AWAY

MARY, we've got a fish, Tom hollered from the cockpit, where he was taking a late afternoon shower.

I recognized the high-pitched whine of the fishing reel, permanently mounted on the stern rail just behind the steering wheel. We dragged the lure behind us whenever we were underway, but rarely caught anything unless we could make at least 4.5 knots. Since leaving the Galapagos a week earlier, we'd been ghosting along in light winds. *Salieri* had struggled to make three knots even with the huge diaphanous black-and-white cruising chute we used for light winds.

Surprised, I raced on deck with the gaff and leather gloves. The sight stopped me dead in my tracks. Braced against the stern rail, his legs in wide stance for balance, trying to reel in the fish, Tom stood stark naked, soap suds in his hair and white foamy lather all over his body.

When he heard my laugh, he grinned, "Holy fuckbubble, this fish is huge. Here," he said, pointing to the reel. "Start pulling him in while I get the gloves on."

"Gawd, this is hard work," I groaned as I tried to wind the crank. "It must be enormous!" As I shifted position to get a better balance, I noticed the speedometer. We were barreling along at 5.5 knots! The wind had enabled us to catch the fish, but to pull it in, I had to overcome a lot of resistance from the water as well as the weight of the fish itself.

"Tom, the wind's gonna blow a hole in the cruising chute," I said. Locking the reel, I unhooked the windvane and took the helm, changing our heading enough to ease the pressure on the sail and slow us down. That would save the sail and make it easier to pull in the fish.

Ten minutes later, Tom had the four-foot tuna close enough to hook the gaff into its gills. "Wow," I crowed. "Sushi for dinner."

Just when Tom had wrestled it to the lifeline where we could pull it into the cockpit, the tuna shook itself violently. We watched in dismay as it flipped off the gaff. As the tuna hit the water, the hook tore out. The fishing line hung limp.

We stared numbly into the water. The muscles around Tom's mouth were trembling, the soap dried and cracking into vertical strings as he swore, "Goddammit to hell. That's the biggest fish we've ever caught...and it got away."

"So did our wind," I moaned. The chute, full of air only moments before, hung as limp as the fishing line. The speedo read 2.5 knots.

I wanted to cry, not about losing dinner—we had plenty of food—but about the ever-growing list of things that, after two weeks at sea, kept going wrong. With the wind from nearly dead astern, *Salieri* wallowed unpredictably, making it a struggle to keep my footing. I sported a rainbow of bruises from banging into the corner of the saloon table or the edge of the galley sink. A coffee cup or cereal bowl left untended for even a moment inevitably slid to the floor.

The nights weren't much better. *Salieri* reverberated with a host of erratic noises—sail blocks banging on the deck, halyards hitting the mast, dishes sliding around in the cupboards. For the past few days, light winds added the slatting of sails to the list of random noises, making sleep a challenge. And when I did manage to fall asleep, our four-hours on/four-hours off watch schedule meant I never got more than three and a half hours at a crack.

To make matters worse, Tom had been experimenting with the sails, trying – generally in vain —to boost our speed. He'd take a sail down and then, an hour later, put the same one back up. An hour after that, he'd take it down one more time and put up a different sail. If the winds were particularly light, he'd set the foresail with a spinnaker pole and then, an hour later, take it down to let the sail fly free.

I thought he was goofy to work that hard to make an extra few miles a day on a five-year cruise, but I knew the sail drills entertained him. Unfortunately, I had to steer whenever he was tinkering with the sails. If he decided to change the sails during his watch at night, he would prod me awake. In a stupor, I would stumble up and take the helm, trying not to fully wake up. I grew crankier with each passing day.

I'd also been unnerved, a few days earlier, when *Pacific*, a yacht we'd first come across in Panama, failed to report in to the daily rollcall on the ham radio net. Several yachties on the net suggested plausible reasons why *Pacific* might not check in—battery problems, fatigue from bad weather, too much partying the night before. But no one knew for sure. To my surprise, no one suggested calling for help.

A wave of panic hit me when *Pacific* didn't answer the roll call the next night. *What if they hit a whale or a submerged container that had fallen off a ship? What if they're drifting in a lifeboat? Pacific's* route, like ours, fell well outside the shipping lanes. For more than a week, we'd seen no signs of civilization—not a ship, not a plane, not a Styrofoam coffee cup, nothing. If they were in a raft without having called for help, the odds of being found after two days of undetermined drifting were perilously small.

I told myself repeatedly there was no reason to panic. We'd often read that whales, while not very bright, were not aggressive. Why would one purposely attack us? And if our path kept us outside the shipping lines, why worry about running into a container? Tom attempted several times to reassure me, pointing out that *Salieri* was in good condition, that we were experienced sailors, that storms were rare at this time of year.

But logic just didn't work. The litany of things to worry about left me constantly jumpy, startled by every unexpected noise. Unable to concentrate enough to read, I tried to focus on fiddly little tasks and played hours of solitaire.

By the time *Pacific* returned to the net the third night, the damage was done. For months, I'd assumed the daily roll call would serve as our safety net, an insurance policy if something went wrong. When no one showed any interest in taking action that second day, I realized how completely on our own Tom and I really were.

Things came to head the night the tuna got away. I had the first watch, from just after dinner until Tom relieved me at 11 p.m.

About 10 minutes later, just after I'd fallen asleep, he nudged me. "Mary, the jenny's limp. Come steer while I set the spinnaker pole."

I felt as if I'd been shot through with a bolt of electricity. Every nerve jangled as I stumbled into the cockpit. The cool night breeze brought goose bumps out on my skin; the red nightlight on the compass pulsed into my retina. Fighting tears, I unhooked the windvane and took the wheel.

When Tom stepped out of the cockpit onto the deck, I panicked. "Tom, put your harness on," I insisted.

"I don't need it. It's a calm night."

"Dammit, we agreed not to go out of the cockpit at night without a harness." My temples throbbed.

"Nothing's gonna happen," he said, making it clear he thought I was making a mountain out of a molehill.

"Tom, if you stumble on a deck cleat, you could trip and fall overboard."

"Mary, stop worrying so much."

I had a sudden image of coming on deck one morning to discover Tom had fallen overboard while I slept. A sob burst out. *I can't do this anymore.* I reset the autopilot and headed below. From the top of the companionway, I swallowed another sob and called out, "Tom, I don't give a damn how fast we go. All I care about is sleep. I'm going to bed." I didn't wait for his response.

When I woke up, my watch showed 5:30 a.m. Tom hadn't wakened me for my 3 a.m. watch. Feeling rested for the first time in weeks, I slid into shorts and a t-shirt, put water on for tea, and went on deck. Tom was asleep, stretched out in the cockpit with his head lolling back on the cabin top, the stopwatch clutched in his left hand. The wind had come up, the sails were full and we were making four knots under a moonlit sky.

I wanted to hug the world.

I sat for a few moments with my hand on Tom's bare leg, flooded by gratitude for his willingness to let me sleep. He looked so gentle, the sweet and funny Tom I'd met on the Vermont ski slope so many years earlier. When I leaned over and kissed his nose, he wrinkled it, but didn't wake up. I kissed him again, this time licking his nose a bit. He opened his eyes and smiled.

"Hi, Mary-pie. Are you feeling better?"

"I can't begin to tell you. But you must be exhausted."

"No, I've dozed quite a bit in the past three hours."

"Isn't that dangerous?" I asked, assuming that it was.

"Nope. I figured out that it takes at least 22 minutes from the time a ship on a collision course appears on the horizon 'til it hits us. So I've set the stopwatch to go off every 19 minutes. That gives me three minutes to adjust our heading—and I only need 30 seconds." He paused. "And we're not in the shipping lanes anyway!"

He started below, but turned back halfway down the steps. "Would you mind if I sleep until I wake up?"

"Go for it. I can't go back to sleep once the sun's up, so I might as well be on watch."

The next night, he took the 7 p.m. watch. Again, he let me sleep. When I woke up a little before 1 a.m., I agreed to take the watch until he woke up.

I dozed with the stopwatch until the yellow-white light began to gather in the eastern sky, ushering in my favorite time of day. For the first time since the Galapagos, I had a sense of being at one with nature, of wanting nothing more than to be exactly where I was.

Just after sunrise, I noticed a black triangular speck on the eastern horizon. I suspected it was Jack and Evelyn on *Melody*, a couple we'd met in the Galapagos. In his mid-40s, Jack looked trim and energetic, an appealing, bear-huggish man with nonstop suggestions for places to see and things to do. Evelyn was quiet, but with a genuine interest in people. Where Jack explained, Evelyn inquired, drawing out even the shiest soul, undaunted by barriers of culture or language. Passionate about music, they had mounted an electronic piano-cum-organ on their saloon bulkhead.

During the weeks we cruised together in the Galapagos, we hiked up and down the goat trails and laughed until our sides ached. Tom and Jack shared boat projects and went spearfishing. Evelyn and I began our shell collections and commiserated about the trials of being married to left-brain men with infinite energy and limited sensitivity. Their daughter, Sara Jane, a spunky little blond, never complained or held us back on the longest of walks or the steepest of climbs.

We'd left the Galapagos for the Marquesas a couple of days before *Melody*, but with their longer hull, expected them to catch up along the way. Two days earlier, when they'd come into VHF range (+/-15 miles), Evelyn called midmorning. "Hi guys. Jack and Sara Jane set the organ up to play Handel's *Messiah* today. If you want to listen in or sing along, switch to Channel 19. We'll leave the mike open." For the next two-and-a-half hours, we listened to the strains of one of world most inspiring musical creations. Tom and I didn't know the music well enough to join Jack and Sara Jane for most of the choral parts, but jumped in enthusiastically for the final Hallelujah chorus. They would never make it to Carnegie Hall, but in mid-ocean, they provided outstanding entertainment.

When Tom woke up around 10 a.m., I called them on the VHF.

"Hi, Mary." Evelyn's cheery voice came through. "There's a boat about 260 degrees from us. Is that you?"

"Yup. I've been watching you since dawn."

"Looks like a nice day for a rendezvous. Jack wants to charge the batteries, so we're gonna crank this baby up enough to reach you by midday."

By noon, they had come alongside. For 10 minutes, we cruised about five yards apart, shouting over the wind and the waves. The conversation, which covered such mundane items as the weather forecast and how long we expected our bananas to last, would have been much easier, but far more prosaic, on the radio. When we ran out of topics, we maneuvered the boats to take each other's picture under full sail.

As they made ready to pull away, Evelyn tossed us a small canvas bag. Jack yelled "... something to do if you get bored." When we opened the bag, we discovered a pornographic coloring book based on *The Joy of Sex* and a box of broken

127

crayons. Jack and Evelyn had already colored the first half of the book. Tom and I spent the afternoon coloring the second half and, to my delight, debating which lovemaking position to try first.

That was a very good day.

In the days that followed, the wind filled in, erratically at first and then more steadily. With the wind up, Tom's need to wring the last inch of forward progress out of the sails diminished. With fewer sail changes, my tolerance for those we did increased. During the day, I began to cook more creatively, no longer undone when a bowl of egg yolks or flour landed on the cabin floor. At night, I studied the constellations of the southern sky, no longer exhausted to the point of tears.

As the days passed, my sense of panic at our isolation eased. As on our Atlantic crossing five years earlier, I couldn't sustain intense fear in the face of ordinary routines—brushing my teeth, doing dishes and mopping the deck. And within a few days, I realized that our inability to control our destiny at sea differed little from our inability to control our life on shore. In New York, we'd harbored the illusion that doctors and ambulances and hospitals could take care of whatever went wrong. At sea, we had no illusions.

This, I mused happily, is what the sailing life is all about.

Chapter 11

On a Lee Shore

STRETCHED out in the cockpit with a book and a cold beer, I heard the powerboats round the headland and roar into the bay. Only a few days earlier, I'd finished reading *Typee,* Melville's novel about the cannibals in the Marquesas a hundred years ago. Although we'd heard nothing about violence in the islands today, my pulse quickened.

Tom was below searching for the source of the leak that had left nearly a foot of water in the bottom of the bilge the day before. "Tom, can you come up?"

His disembodied voice responded. "...something wrong?"

"Four big power boats are heading straight for us."

"I'm on my way."

By the time he got up on deck, the four 25-foot runabouts had powered past us, their beefy Tongan crews waving cheerily. The boats, all with 500 HP engines, were magnificent, their polished hulls lacquered in the lustrous tones of dark red or green I associated with the Corvettes of my youth. They looked well-loved.

They powered another 100 yards into the narrow bay and anchored about 30 feet off shore, just this side of the surf breaking on the beach. Holding their shotguns over their heads, they waded ashore and disappeared into the jungle.

"…probably hunting goats." Tom said as he went below to continue his search for the leak.

Watching the runabouts silhouetted against the surf, I recalled our own trip ashore earlier that afternoon, in search of a stream rumored to be filled with freshwater shrimp. "Who knows," Jack said as he proposed yet another adventure, "We might find dinner."

Struggling to steer his dinghy through unexpectedly large waves, Jack cruised parallel to the beach for several minutes, trying to find a break in the surf. When he saw an opportunity, he turned the bow in toward shore, but the calm was too short-lived. A following wave broke over our stern, drenching us all. When the dinghy hit another steep swell and nearly capsized, Tom and Jack jumped into the water and managed to haul the dinghy ashore.

Strolling single-file along the sandy jungle path, we found a burbling waterfall surrounded with fruit trees, the air thick with a cloyingly sweet smell we couldn't identify. The fresh water was thick with shrimp but they looked too tiny, I thought, to be worth harvesting for dinner. Jack scrabbled to fill a bucket of shrimp for *Melody* while Evelyn and I gathered bananas, limes and guava.

As I hoisted up my fully loaded backpack, Jack predictably suggested, "Let's see how far the path goes. The jungle doesn't seem too thick."

Their nodding heads confirmed that Tom and Sara Jane were game for a hike, but Evelyn wailed, "Jack, enough already. It's late. I don't want to fight the surf in the dark. Let's come back in the morning."

"Just a little way, honey. Com'on," he pleaded.

Worried about the leak in the bilge, I chimed in. "I vote

for the morning." Tom had pumped the water out, but without knowing where the leak was, I hesitated to leave *Salieri* for too long.

"You guys are no damn fun at all," Jack pouted as we tromped back to the beach. I noticed Tom turn toward Jack and roll his eyes in sympathy. Once on the beach, Evelyn, Sara Jane and I waded into the surf and climbed into the dinghy. The guys had to tow us beyond the surf before they could safely hoist themselves in.

The next morning the runabouts remained at anchor. With no signs of life from *Melody* or Tom, I made coffee and settled in the cockpit to read. After only a few minutes, however, I put my book down. As much as I loved reading, I'd done a lot more of it in the Marquesas than I'd planned. The islands, nothing like the seafaring, communal culture described by Herman Melville and Jack London, had been a disappointment.

True, our first glimpse of the steep volcanic peaks soaring up from the water's edge, after 28 days at sea, thrilled me. But the closer we got to Atuona, our first port of call, the greater my disappointment in a world about which we had such grand expectations. Instead of woven pandanus walls, we saw houses of painted cinderblock. Instead of handmade thatch, we saw roofs of corrugated iron, a few brightly painted, most unpainted and rusty. As we came into the inner harbor, we threaded our way through a fleet of power boats rather than the beautiful outrigger canoes we'd been led to expect.

Once ashore, my disappointment mounted. The women—big boned, heavy, and dressed in the colorful *pareos* made famous by Gauguin paintings—wore western-style bras with the straps showing. Instead of open-air markets with bread-fruit, guava and fresh fish, air-conditioned grocery stores stocked New Zealand butter and French cheese. As we strolled into town, Peugeots and Datsuns passed us regularly.

Contact with island residents proved equally unsatisfying.

The French, predictably reluctant to speak English, tended to be abrupt and dismissive if asked for directions. The locals, more willing to offer advice and generous with gifts of fresh food, knew less about the history and culture of their islands than we did. The one exception was the absence of any way to say "thank you" in the Marquesan tongue, which traced to the island's history as a communal society. Gradually we came to understand that that the expression "thank you" developed in the western world as a response to the receipt of something one had no right to have or any necessary expectation of receiving. In a communal society, where what's yours is mine and what's mine is yours, the phrase serves no social function.

While we did enjoy hiking along the goat trails that laced the magnificent mountainsides, most of the bays were too deep or murky for snorkeling. We often went for days without seeing another cruising yacht and I missed the variety of activities and companionship I'd had in Panama. To make matters worse, Tom and I both developed an undiagnosed skin rash that itched like crazy. Despite the awe-inspiring landscape, we had decided to make our way through the Marquesas as expeditiously as we could.

Now, anchored in Hana Menu, a small bay on the north shore of Hiva Oa, I watched the beautiful boats pitching violently in the surf. Wondering why the surf ran so high with almost no wind, I worried about how much longer their anchors could hold.

Opening the hatch over the forward berth, I called down to Tom. "Hey, kiddo, wake up. The surf is way up, much worse than last night. I'm afraid the runabouts are gonna break loose from their anchors. We need to do something."

Groggily, Tom stood up on the berth. Frowning, he shook his head. "I don't know what we can do. Our dinghy would get swamped in a heartbeat." Even as he spoke, the boat closest to the beach rose high on a wave, pitched end-over-end and crashed upside down on the sand, its propeller spinning uselessly in the air.

"*Salieri*, this is *Melody*. Come in *Salieri*." Jack's voice sounded shrill.

Tom picked up the mike. "*Salieri* here. Hi, Jack."

"Tom, did you see that boat crash on the beach? We've got to do something."

"Hey, the surf's worse now than last night. I don't think we can do anything."

"I guess you're right. I feel bad, though. I wish we could help. *Melody* out."

He called back barely a minute later, as usual, with a plan. "Since we can't go ashore, we're gonna leave for Taiohae later this morning."

"I just woke up. Let me talk to Mary. Maybe we'll go with you."

As I handed Tom a cup of steaming coffee, I said, "I'm okay with going to Taiohae. If we can't go ashore, we might as well use the day to travel. By the way, did you ever find the leak?"

"Nope." He grabbed a flashlight, pulled up a floorboard and peered into the bilge. "Dry as a bone. Curious. We took on so much water yesterday. Must be something with the engine."

Over breakfast, we decided to leave for Taiohae and try to identify the source of the leak as we traveled. When Tom went on deck to switch on the engine, another runabout had landed on the beach.

A few minutes later, as I finished up breakfast dishes, Tom said, "Gees, Mary, you must have been flinging dishwater around like crazy."

I looked up, expecting a humorous jibe of some sort. "What are you gabbling about now?"

He pointed down, near the edge of the galley sink. "Look at the puddle."

"I didn't do that," I retorted in mock offense.

With a wary look on his face, he lifted the floorboard to find the bilge full of water. "Damn, it was dry 20 minutes ago." He flipped the bilge pump on and then pulled the heavy wooden cover off the engine. There it was, a steady stream of salt water, like a little boy pissing into a sandbox, spurting from a pencil-sized hole in the salt-water cooling system.

"Turn off the engine, quick," he said.

Racing up to the cockpit, I sighed, weary of the never-ending saga of things that go wrong on a boat. When I got the engine off, I plopped down on the top step of the companionway, just above where Tom huddled over the engine. "So… can you fix it?"

Tom gave me his best Popeye pose, his right arm flexed in the air. "Oh, you faithless creature! Of course I can. I've got my magic metal epoxy for just this purpose."

I burst out laughing. How I envied Tom his ability to find humor in the most trying situations.

By the time he finished the repair, well before noon, the breaking surf had moved about 40 yards out from shore. The last of those gorgeous runabouts had upended on the beach. The long swells rolling up under *Salieri* and *Melody* made me a little nauseous.

Tom called *Melody*. "Hi, Jack. I've fixed the leak, but the epoxy won't be dry enough to run the engine until 5 p.m. We'll leave for Taiohae when it's dry."

"We'll wait," Jack said companionably. "Let's play scrabble."

"You don't need to sit around all day. We'll be fine. We'll meet you in Taiohae this evening."

The VHF went dead for a minute and then Jack came back. "Evelyn and I agree. We're not leaving you alone without an engine. That surf is just too weird."

"That's nice of you," Tom replied. "Can we buy you lunch for your troubles?"

Evelyn came on, obviously elbowing Jack out of the way. "Such a deal! What can I bring?"

"How about some fresh bread?" I suggested. My culinary skills, I'd discovered, did not include the ability to make bread that anyone would want to eat. Even hot from the oven, my bread generally tasted like day-old cardboard.

By the time we'd finished lunch—chorizo from Panama, freshly made cole slaw, Evelyn's just-baked bread, and home-made yogurt with bananas—the surf was breaking more than halfway between us and the beach. The growing swells now lifted us up and down a full six feet, three feet on either side of the 30-foot depth when we anchored. By 2:30, the line of waves broke less than 20 yards from our bow. Each time we rose to the top of a swell, our anchor chain went taut, clanking loudly.

Jack and Evelyn dinghied back to *Melody*, reluctant to leave her unattended in the roiling water. As they left, Tom said, "If you want to get out of here, we won't mind. These swells are hard on your anchor chain."

Jack sounded firm. "Tom, we're not leaving without you. Period. We'll put our engine in low gear to take some strain off the chain. We'll be fine."

Just before 4 p.m., the surf broke under our bow for the first time. Both sailboats pitched violently. Each time the anchor chain went taut, *Salieri* shuddered. Swells crashing on the walls of the narrow bay created secondary waves that washed over our deck from the side.

As Tom staggered to the bow to check the anchor yet again, I wondered how much longer we had before the chain snapped. I doubted we could last for another hour. When Tom came back to the cockpit, the muscles in his back and neck were ropy from tension. "Mary, we're outta here. If the epoxy doesn't hold, we'll figure out what to do once we're out of the bay. Call *Melody* while I turn the engine on."

Once again, Jack had an idea. "We'll up anchor first and

wait for you under power. If your engine doesn't work, we can throw you a line and tow you out of the bay."

"Thanks, Jack. But I think we're okay. The epoxy seems to be holding."

With the engine in gear, I moved *Salieri* forward enough to take the strain off the anchor. The shudder stopped but we still pitched as if we were beating into a heavy sea. I gasped with shock as a towering wave of water came over the starboard side, drenching me and filling the cockpit. Some of the water flew down the companionway, where Tom had just replaced the engine cover.

"Holy shit, what was that?" Tom screeched.

"Water," I said, not very helpfully. "Are you okay?"

"Yes, but a minute sooner and we would have had salt water all over the engine."

Wiping his head with a towel as he came up, he muttered. "Let's get this baby outta here."

To our surprise, we found the open sea outside the bay calm, almost mirror-like, with hardly enough wind to justify raising the sails. But most remarkable of all, as we came around the headland, we saw *Melody*'s bow nearly touching the seaward end of a huge rainbow.

I called Evelyn. "So, what's it like at the end of the rainbow? Can you see the pot of gold?"

She laughed. "Don't I wish? But, Mary the rainbow's way off to the east of us."

"Well," I pointed out, "You're east of us and from our vantage point, you're right smack dab at the end of it." I paused. "You know, Evelyn, I would have been terrified this afternoon if we'd been alone. I can't tell you how grateful I am that you stayed with us."

"Don't give it a thought. But if you want to pay us back, get a picture of us at the end of the rainbow."

"It's a deal."

Many months later, we learned we'd sat through the early stages of a tidal wave caused by an underwater volcanic eruption in the Pacific Ocean, a thousand miles to the north. The tidal wave peaked about six hours after we left. We had no way of knowing what would have happened to us had we stayed in the long, narrow bay that funneled and magnified the force of the underwater reverberations. I can't imagine it would have been good.

We'd originally gravitated to the sailing life because we loved working with nature rather than trying to control it. We understood in a visceral way that, in this environment, our fate depended on a host of things ultimately outside our control. Even so, the experience in Hana Menu provided a sobering reminder of the limits of our control over our existence. For months, it took my breath away to realize how close we'd come to disaster without even realizing it.

Chapter 12

The Fearsome
Foursome

L OOK, Tom…aren't they beautiful? Do you suppose they've come to take us in?" Several times before, as we'd approached coral passes in the Marquesas and the Tuamotus, dolphins had appeared outside the reef and guided us to safety inside the lagoon.

Tom had the wheel as we paralleled the reef that enclosed Opunohu Bay in Moorea. He'd maintained a safe distance from the wall of foam and spray where the ocean waves crashed on the rocky coral. I sat perched on the cabin top, searching for the patch of calm water that marked the entrance to the Bay.

Suddenly, the water broke as a dozen dolphins burst through the surface in graceful arcs on our starboard side. Delighted, I could see five more of the sleek beasts cavorting in front of us, their powerful fins keeping them just ahead of the bow wave. Dolphins, according to sailing lore, bring good luck.

They frolicked alongside *Salieri* for a few minutes and

then veered sharply off toward the reef, all of them at once. I signaled to Tom to follow their trail. Within minutes, the break in the reef appeared. The dolphins led us through the pass, but once we were safely in the long, narrow lagoon, they disappeared as suddenly as they'd arrived.

I pointed Tom toward a patch of shallow water at a healthy distance from the one boat already at anchor. Within 15 minutes, we'd set the anchor and I was stretched out in the cockpit, soaking up the scenery. Soaring mountains that drop to the water's edge were a familiar sight in the Pacific, but the vista here—lush, green hills towering above us with the jagged peak of Mt. Rotui grey-green in the distance—was spectacular even by Pacific standards. I watched with fascination as a family of goats traipsed across the face of a breathtakingly steep hill. I couldn't fathom why they didn't slither down the hill, en masse, into the water below.

Handing me a cold beer, Tom smiled. "What bit of good luck do you s'pose the dolphins brought us this time?"

Distracted, I returned his smile. Out of the corner of my eye, I'd noticed a gray-and-yellow dinghy heading toward us, its driver sporting a mass of platinum blond hair and a skimpy avocado-colored wraparound affair that looked like it came from a shop on Rodeo Drive. She put the engine in neutral as she came alongside. Her greeting bubbled with laughter.

"Welcome to Moorea. I'm Salli Page on *Last Act*. I brought you a ripe papaya. We've got more than we can eat before they go bad." She handed the fruit to Tom. "...And you are?"

Almost before he'd given our names, she peppered us with more questions. "Where are you from? Where are you heading? How long have you been cruising? Where did you stay in Tahiti? I want to hear everything." Her breathless queries tumbled out.

When she finally paused, Tom reached out his hand. "Why don't you come aboard?"

She joined us in the cockpit, but shook her head when Tom offered a beer. "I can't stay long. Tell me about you."

As Tom gave her the three-minute version of our New York background and sailing route, Salli's eyes opened wide. "Wow, we left San Francisco only three months ago, but it seems like forever. Do you still like it after nearly two years?"

I chimed in. "Some days yes, some days no. I loved the Bahamas, but I was disappointed by the Marquesas."

Salli turned to me. "Why? What didn't you like, Mary?"

Tom jumped in before I could reply. "Tell us about you and Dan."

I gave him an evil look, my first reaction fury that he would cut me off so rudely. Within moments, however, I realized that, since leaving Panama, I'd settled back into my old habit of letting Tom take the lead with strangers. My desire to talk to Salli, far more than his interruption, reflected the change in circumstances.

Salli seemed not to notice, however, as she bubbled out their story. "We're heading to Kiwi country. My husband Dan's a senior IBM manager. I've been in sales and interior design for 15 years, selling office furniture to Silicon Valley. I was in the right place at the right time, made a bundle, and decided to take a break. Dan wangled an 18-month leave of absence, but we have to go back." She barely paused for breath. "Well, I'm off. I'm sure you guys have stuff to do."

I liked her vitality. It occurred to me that she and Dan might have a story not unlike ours. As she started up the dinghy engine, I called out to her, "Why don't you come for drinks later? The sun comes over the yard-arm by five or so...does that work for you?"

She waved as she headed off. "Absolutely. We'll see you later."

When they returned, Dan proved to be every bit as classy as Salli, tall and trim, with a lush salt-and-pepper beard. But where Salli effervesced, he was quiet and understated.

Although he responded amiably to our questions, he seldom took any conversational initiative.

Our conversation that evening covered the standard biographical stuff…schools, jobs, sailing experiences, cruising itineraries. Although they now lived in California, they too came originally from the Midwest. Like us, they were a two-career couple, hardworking and successful, who'd broken away from the "fast track" in order to experience another dimension of life while they were still fit and healthy. Like us, they were experienced sailors who'd suffered through a demoralizing stream of accidents and mechanical failures during their first few months.

We learned that they'd met Jack and Evelyn in Tahiti and shared our sense of both exhilaration and exhaustion that came from trying to keep pace with Jack as he raced up one hill and down another. And in the truly 'small world' department, Dan and Salli had been on the 1970 Mackinac–Chicago race, a highlight of Tom's youthful sailing career.

As I lay waiting to fall asleep that night, I realized the evening had been the first time I'd felt completely at ease with another cruising couple. I had an instinctive sense of kinship, an unfamiliar confidence that they found me interesting, a certainty that I wanted to get to know them. A door had opened, letting a burst of fresh air into my life.

Over the next few days, the four of us hiked up the goat trail to the top of Mt. Rotui and explored a number of marae, the abandoned Polynesian temples whose sacred meaning had been lost when measles and syphilis, brought by the Spaniards, wiped out centuries of oral history and tradition. Several evenings, we shared potluck suppers, expanding our conversation to include lifestyles, politics, religion and reading preferences.

A classic extrovert, Salli possessed boundless energy and a perpetual good humor. Like Tom, she always had an amusing story to fill a lull in the conversation. Like Tom, she was always up for an adventure, long after my energy level had dropped to nil. Like me, she'd begun a shell collection and spent many hours investigating local mores and styles. She and I spent many hours poking around village markets and low-tide reefs when Dan and Tom were snorkeling or absorbed in boat projects.

Dan seemed the polar opposite of Salli—moody and a bit misanthropic, his darkness relieved by a wry, self-deprecating sense of humor. One night, over dessert, he read us, item by item, his list of 20 questions, the prompts he relied on to get through unavoidable social interaction, to get him past the awkward moments when a conversation seemed moribund. His questions struck me as banal—"Do you have children?" "Where else have your sailed?" "What did you do for a living?"—and he provoked near mockery when he told us he reviewed them each time he had to participate in a group activity. Even as I laughed, I felt a burst of empathy. It struck me that it was as hard for him to make conversation with strangers as it was for me, that he relied on Salli the same way I relied on Tom.

Dan also seemed fiercely independent. While he often volunteered to help Tom sort out mechanical or electronic problems on *Salieri*, he never asked for Tom's advice or assistance on *Last Act*.

Several days later, we sailed through the pass at Faré, the largest village on the tiny island of Huahine. As we steered toward the dense cluster of yachts near shore, Salli dinked over. "We're over on the shoal," she called out, pointing to *Last Act* alone in the center of the harbor. There's plenty of room by us."

A few hours after we dropped our hook near *Last Act*, we picked Dan and Salli up in our dinghy and went ashore to explore the annual Fête activities. On the dock, we met up with *Melody* and began a leisurely tour of the palm-frond stalls, bedecked with croton and bougainvillea. The locally-made batik *pareos*—the flat length of cloth, wrapped much like a bath towel, that the local women wear for everyday dress— were mouthwatering, but even more expensive than in Tahiti. By contrast, the carved wooden figures fell well below the standard we'd seen on other islands. While the food stalls offered local cuisine —pork, parrot fish, yams, breadfruit—they struck us as bland, as if prepared for a tourist palate.

Over dinner, we agreed that the Fête had been disappointing. Jack, of course, primed us for the next adventure. "There's a big bay at the south end of Huahine, one you can get to inside the reef. Evelyn and I are going there tomorrow morning. Why don't you guys join us?"

"I'd love to get out of here," Dan chimed in at once. "This place feels like a trailer park."

Early the next afternoon, we took the inner channel up to Baie d'Avea where we anchored in 10 feet of water so still and clear we seemed to be floating on air. The brilliant, white sand below us, carved into long, curving ripples by the tidal flow, was littered with giant, black sea cucumbers, starfish in both orange and neon blue, along with a sea urchin garbed in red spines as thick as your finger. Even from up on deck, we could see the mollusk trails in the sand, the path where the tiny animals moved across the seabed. On the beach, nestled under the palm trees, sat the Relais Mahana, a guest house with a large terrace perfect for watching the ever-so-brief "green flash" as the tropical sun set over the lagoon.

The six of us met for drinks on the terrace at sunset and then gathered on *Last Act* for a potluck supper. Afterwards, we played the dictionary game until nearly midnight. Evelyn won, hands down, with the word "eryngo," which none of us recognized but which we all, coincidentally, defined in terms of some disfiguring disease. When we'd laughed ourselves sick at each other's goofy definitions, Evelyn informed us it was, in fact, "a sea holly whose roots had aphrodisiac properties." We exploded with laughter all over again.

The next night, we held our potluck on *Melody*, where Jack and Sara Jane played songs from the '60s and we sang ourselves hoarse. We congratulated ourselves on our good fortune in having the anchorage to ourselves, Dan dismissing "all those silly sheep huddled together in Fare." Sara Jane, obviously comfortable with the group, decided to spend the night on *Salieri*.

I relished the lazy days of biking, windsurfing and snorkeling. In that setting, conversation came easily to me. I groaned inwardly on the fourth day when *Elixir* sailed into the bay. While we'd all met Stan and Jessie, no one knew much about them and their arrival felt like an invasion. But it seemed inhospitable to let them eat alone while our three boats partied into the night, so we invited them to join us for drinks and dinner. As it turned out, they too were midlife professionals taking a break. A high-energy, "type A" couple, they had become members in good standing of our little clan by the end of the evening.

A few days later, the four boats reluctantly returned to Faré to buy fresh fruit and bread. We planned to celebrate Bastille Day in Bora Bora, with stops at several smaller islands along the way. The four boats maintained radio contact throughout each day; most nights found the four boats anchored in the same bay. Typically, we did potluck picnics on the beach, talking late into the night. When conversation failed, we piled onto *Melody* to make music. I could always find someone willing to go snorkeling, to hold a wrench, or to come up with the one missing ingredient in a recipe. It seemed the best of all possible worlds.

"*Salieri*, this is *Last Act*. Come in, *Salieri*."

Tom grabbed the VHF. "Hi, Dan. Where are you? We thought you'd be here by now."

"We're on our way to Tahaa. But we got a late start and won't get there until just before dusk." A long pause. "Ummh… that's why I'm calling. I'll stand you and Mary to banana daiquiris if you'll talk us in."

Tom shook his head as if to refuse, but he actually said "of course." Another pause. "…but only 'cuz you offered daiquiris."

I listened with a sinking feeling. We'd struggled to thread the narrow serpentine channel into the anchorage even with the midday sun highlighting the coral beneath the surface. Now, with the sun low in the sky, we'd have to guide them through, based on our faulty memory of distances between turns in an unmarked channel.

The responsibility was daunting. But we couldn't leave them to sail in circles all night outside the anchorage. Then, too, we didn't want to turn down Dan's first request for help.

When *Last Act* arrived, Tom radioed instructions, giving landmarks for each successive turn in the channel. All went well until the last leg, a deep and particularly narrow slot with shallow rocks on either side. "Dan, point your bow at *Salieri*. That'll give you a straight shot in."

Even as Tom spoke, a wind shift caused *Salieri* to swing toward shore. Dan didn't realize we'd moved and so aimed straight for the rocks. I grabbed the radio to warn him to head left, but another boat was using the public frequency. From the deck, I heard Tom shout across the water, but he was too late. With 90 feet of water under her stern, *Last Act's* bow was solidly wedged in the coral.

We raced over to lend assistance. The folks on *Melody* and *Elixir* followed close behind. Using lines cleated amidships on *Last Act*, several of us braced ourselves against trees on either side of the channel and tried to rock her from side to side. As she pivoted, Tom and Jack, using lines tied to her stern, inched her backwards into deep water. By the time we pulled *Last Act* off the ledge and got her safely anchored in the cove, darkness had fallen.

Dan stood all three boats to those daiquiris and made them strong enough to kill any embarrassment Tom and I felt. As we sat around re-embellishing the tale from our differing perspectives, we took pride in having worked as a team to get *Last Act* afloat. It was Dan, on the third round of daiquiris, who observed "that was a fearsome sight, watching you all get this huge boat off the rocks."

Thus was born the Fearsome Foursome, my family for the next three months.

CHAPTER 13

PARADISE FOUND

A FTER 10 days at sea, we arrived in the archipelago of Vava'u in the kingdom of Tonga. Since we had arrived too late in the day to navigate the circuitous entry channel into Neiafu, the administrative center of Vava'u, we anchored nearby in Vaitutaka Bay. As dusk settled in, Tom and I watched the lengthening shadows cast by the setting sun on the steeply wooded shore. With almost no breeze, *Salieri* sat nearly motionless.

For no particular reason, I looked down into the water. "Tom, look," I gasped, pointing into the water.

There, 60 feet below, we could see every detail of the ocean floor, the jagged rocks, the blue and yellow fish, the huge coral fans in shades of purple, yellow and orange undulating in the deeper currents. We watched spellbound until the night stole away our view.

The next morning, we made our way to Neiafu, the vast, completely enclosed crater of a volcano that had sunk into the sea eons before. The town center, a long row of single-story white clapboard buildings with green shutters, sat high on a bluff overlooking the harbor. We had just sailed into the pages of a British colonial history book.

The experience of Tonga was unlike anything that had come before. For nearly two years, we'd progressed from one place on our itinerary to the next in sequential fashion, each memory slotted in its correct relationship to the one that came before and the one that came after.

By contrast, my memories of Tonga are vivid but jumbled. We held picnics on the beach. We walked along the low-tide reef. We attended Sunday church services. What I don't remember is which beach, which reef, which church connected to which island. Without my journal, I can't recall the order in which most events occurred.

I suspect it is because every trip began and ended in Neiafu. Immigration authorities required cruisers to have permits to visit the outer islands. Since they rarely gave approval for more than five or six islands at a time, we returned to Neiafu periodically for a new permit. As a result, we cruised out from the hub of an imaginary wheel, along the spokes to the rim and then back again. I have trouble distinguishing one set of islands from another in any chronological sense.

But the explanation I prefer is that, during our six weeks in Tonga, we had no fixed destination. Some days, we planned to move to a new anchorage, but never quite got around to it. Other days, we headed for a given cove, but changed our plans halfway, often because one of the Fearsome Foursome called to say they'd found a particularly appealing spot. Our planning horizon rarely extended beyond the next meal.

One of those recurring memories is day-sailing for the sheer pleasure of it. Tom first brought up the idea as we sipped morning coffee, watching the sunrise. Playing on an old joke, he said, "Well, Mary-pie, another boring day in Paradise."

Amused by the now-familiar image, I responded with my oft-used line, "I think I can handle the stress."

"I have an idea..." His voice trailed off.

"And I bet you want me to ask you what it is."

"Let's go sailing." A boyish grin lit up his face.

I laughed out loud. "Sailing? We live on a boat. We sail all the time."

"But we always sail to get someplace. It's been months since we went sailing for the pure pleasure of it."

"It's a gorgeous day. Let's do it."

Tom's smile broadened. Sauntering to the foredeck, he hit the toggle on the electric windlass with his foot, just enough to pull the slack out of the anchor line. *Salieri* inched forward. He ambled back and went below. A few minutes later, he emerged with a book and went forward. Sitting on the cabin top, he toggled the windlass several times, each time pulling in the slack that had formed in the intervening minutes. Each time, *Salieri* moved forward another few feet. Between toggles, he read.

Watching from the cockpit, I realized how much Tom had changed! The man with the book bore little resemblance to the man who, only six months earlier, had insisted on sailing dead down in a heavy sea just to avoid losing a few hours in a 10-day journey. Sailing with Tom no longer frightened me. I trusted him completely.

Ten minutes later, he hollered out. "Mary, the anchor's off the bottom. The weight of the anchor is all that's holding us in place. We're ready to go."

As Tom started to haul up the mainsail, I took both the wheel and the line controlling the shape of the mainsail.

"Tom, do you want the engine on?"

"Nah, let's just float on outta here!"

Which we did.

When Tom had the main raised all the way, I let the boom swing outboard. *Salieri* began to coast forward. Tom came back and took the mainsheet as I steered us out of the bay. When we got to open water, we pulled the last few feet of the anchor chain onto the deck.

For several glorious hours, we cruised around the islands and then returned to the spot where we'd started that morning. Coming back, we repeated the routine in reverse, dropping the anchor a few feet into the water just before entering the bay. Once in the bay, I pulled the main in toward the centerline to slow us down. Our forward motion stopped right where we wanted to drop the anchor. Once we'd set the hook, we dropped the mainsail on the deck.

After furling the sail, Tom wandered over to where I stood in the cockpit, putting on the instrument covers. Wrapping his arm around my shoulder, he kissed the top of my head. "What a great day," he exclaimed. "Do you realize we never turned the engine on? Do you s'pose we've finally learned how to sail?"

In that moment, I fell in love with Tom all over again.

A newfound intimacy colored our days, during even the most pedestrian of activities.

As part of our daily routine, we had to decide whether to have fresh food for dinner or pull something out of the ship's stores. We continued to drag the fishing line, but our luck varied. When we wanted shell fish—clams, mussels, oysters— our menu depended on whether low tide occurred in time for us to gather food and prepare it.

One gorgeous afternoon, we lay at anchor off the leeward beach of a deserted island. Having been told that clams and mussels were thick on the windward beach, I had visions of paella for dinner.

Ambling over to where Tom lay stretched out on the cabin top under the awning, reading, I grabbed his big toe and shook it. "Hey, buddy," I said. "How about a walk on the beach to get clams or mussels for dinner?"

He peered at me over the top of his book. "Okay. Shall we swim ashore? I can make it back with the clam bag when it's full."

"You got the job," I said, happy to get the extra exercise.

Tom tied the clam bag and small shovel around his waist, and we swam the 30 yards to shore in the clear warm water, checking out the orange and yellow coral heads below as we moved along the surface. Tucking our flippers and snorkel masks under a hibiscus bush, we strolled across the narrow island toward the expanse of damp sand on the far beach.

For several minutes, we sat on the sand and watched the surf breaking heavily on the far edge of reef, about 30 yards away. I had come to love the sound of the waves spilling onto the beach, deep and resonant, yet reminiscent of breaking glass, a sound that you could hear in your ears and feel in your feet. As we strolled along the beach looking for places to dig, Tom reached for my hand, entwining his fingers in mine, slowly caressing them. I felt his presence, his body and his heart, in a way that had never occurred in New York, even in the earliest days of our courtship. We strolled hand-in-hand, our pace ever slower, as we paused to comment on a sand formation, a shell that had washed up, or crab scuttling across the beach. He never let go of my hand.

A quarter-mile down the beach, his fingers began to circle slowly around my palm. I moved my hand to encourage him. A quarter-mile after that, we sat down to watch a colony of hermit crabs, squatters in bleached-out seashells long since abandoned by their original owners. As we watched, Tom released my hand and began to stroke my neck and my back, his fingers tracing a line along my skin just below the edge of my bathing suit. I felt affection as much as desire.

We made love on the warm damp sand, to the sound of screeching gulls and crashing waves. After 15 years, it was making love, not just having sex. That evening, back on board *Salieri*, we feasted on the mussels and clams, broiled with garlic and butter. As Tom reached out with his fork to put a mussel in my mouth, I decided it was the best seafood I ever tasted.

One of my favorite routines was walking with Salli on a low tide beach, inspecting the tidal pools and hunting for shells.

Before the sailing trip, I'd never been a collector of anything, but shells had become a passion in the months since the Galapagos, a passion Salli and I shared. The variety of shells seemed infinite, in the way that flower varieties are infinite. I made it a point never to take a live mollusk—most countries had laws against it anyway. But I learned early on that a shell only washed up on the beach when its original inhabitant had died. In that sparsely populated corner of the world, it was easy to be the first person to arrive after a beautiful shell washed up.

Between our explorations of tidal pools we talked, mostly about everyday stuff—new recipes, a proposed anchorage or the latest gossip about one of the many sailing couples crossing the Pacific that year. Occasionally, when the tide and weather were right, we talked about life before cruising.

As we talked, we discovered a shared experience in having self-absorbed and hypercritical mothers. We compared our experiences as professionals in a man's world, congratulating ourselves on our good fortune in being married to men who weren't threatened by successful women. We commiserated about being childless, but recognized that the financial obligations of educating children would almost certainly have precluded this remarkable adventure that had brought the two of us together. During those leisurely walks, I had the time and inclination to talk to another woman in ways I had never felt free to do before. From Salli, I began to learn a whole new language of friendship.

One of our most memorable walks took place on the outer reef near Ofu where *Last Act* and *Salieri* had anchored near a row of pastel-painted houses behind a crystal white beach that ran the length of the island. A Sunday, we were loathe to swim or snorkel off the boat, out of respect for the islanders who spent the Sabbath in prayer and contemplation. We learned early on that they took offense when cruisers disrupted the quiet of the day.

Never particularly religious, Tom and I had begun to go to Sunday services as, along with the market, the churches were integral to the Tongan social structure. That morning, we'd attended services at the Methodist Church on the island. When Salli called to go for a walk, I was shaving one of my last cabbages for coleslaw. Glad for something active to do, I agreed to pick her up in 20 minutes.

When I banged on *Last Act's* hull, Salli appeared on deck. For the umpteenth time, I wondered how anyone living on a cruising boat could look so glamorous. Her shorts were never wrinkled, her tank tops never faded or stretched. Her blond mane looked like she'd just put the blow drier away. She might be a friend, but at that moment, in my unironed seersucker sunsuit and drip-dry hair, I absolutely hated her.

As she scrambled down into the dinghy, I heard an unfamiliar note in her greeting, the sound of frustration. "I'm going nuts, Mary. Dan's boat projects never seem to end. A walk will do me good." Given her normal good humor, I was concerned.

We planed across the bay and anchored a few meters from the reef. Wading ashore, we assembled a pile of new shells—three deer cowries, a couple of cones and two miters—and then headed to the ocean side of the reef where the pounding waves kept the marine life active in hundreds of small pools. We found one pool full of small blue-black limpets, another with several deer cowries, a third thick with miniature red crabs scuttling back and forth. One unusually deep pool held a magnificent albino cowrie, nearly as big as my fist, with its owner's fleshy body, very much alive, wrapped around the outer edges. We looked at it longingly and moved on.

I returned to our earlier conversation. "So, what's Dan working on? Is something wrong with the boat?"

Salli's response was tart. "Not a damn thing, as near as I can tell. It's part of his daily maintenance routine—this time it's the fuel pump. I know it has to be done, but I don't believe it takes as much time as he says he needs. Mary, I've spent far too much of this trip waiting for him to finish some task on that damned boat."

I grimaced, remembering *Salieri's* early days on the ICW. "I've been there, kiddo. I know how you feel."

"Really?" She looked at me, her head cocked to one side. "Tom's so outgoing. It never occurred to me that he'd look for reasons to avoid people."

I wondered if maybe I didn't understand. "Oh, Tom wasn't trying to avoid people. He's much too sociable. But so many things on the boat were going wrong. The pressure took its toll." I paused, "You certainly had your share of boat problems in the first few months. If Dan's at all like Tom, he probably takes his responsibility way too seriously."

"You can say that again!" she agreed. "But, gees, Mary, Dan absolutely uses boat projects to avoid socializing. It's left me on my own a lot more than I expected to be."

Her comment puzzled me. "I know Dan is always joking about being antisocial, but I sure haven't seen much evidence of that."

She shrugged. "He likes you and Tom…and Jack and Evelyn. But he doesn't have much patience for most of the other cruisers. And he's just not comfortable in groups."

"Well, I sympathize with him, Salli. I spent most of the first year of this trip feeling like I had nothing to say and no one to talk to except Tom. We went to barbecues and did potlucks and hiked, but I always found it hard to make conversation. Until we met *Melody*, I never got beyond the level of acquaintance with anyone."

Salli stared at me. "But you're not antisocial."

"Maybe antisocial is too strong, but being with people I don't know well is exhausting. It feels like work. That's why I love Dan's 20 questions. I need them as much as he does."

"You could have fooled me!"

"It's not work being with you," I replied.

She stopped and gave me a hug. "Well, having you guys and *Melody* has made a huge difference for me. I'm dreading the return trip."

"I thought you planned to ship *Last Act* back to San Fran from Australia."

"We had planned to. But it's shockingly expensive and Dan wants to sail back." I could see her blinking back tears. "I don't think I can do it, Mary. The trip out was so terrible… being constantly seasick."

"Did you try patches or Dramamine?"

"Nothing worked. Between San Francisco and the Marquesas, I got seasick whenever it got rough. And then I was sick all the way from Bora Bora to Nuie. Mary, I'm not looking forward to the 10-day trip to New Zealand." She hesitated, scrunching up her mouth. "I haven't told him yet that I want to fly back. He's going to be really upset."

"But won't he understand if he's seen you so sick?"

"I guess. But even if I meet him in Hawaii, we'll be apart for nearly six months. Mary, we're much more dependent on each other than you and Tom. Neither Dan or I manage very well alone."

Salli's comment surprised me. "Why do you think being apart from Tom would be easier for me?"

Salli paused, chewing on her lower lip. "I hope I'm not out of line here, but it seems like you both want to do your own thing. Neither of you wants advice or suggestions from the other. You haggle all the time...about who's going to tell the story...who's going to decide the menu...who knows the recipe best. It's good-humored enough, but it feels like underneath your words, you're always competing."

I recoiled at the picture she painted. Learning to work as a team had been a hard-won achievement and I knew there were still some rough edges. But I had never seen Tom and me as competitors.

"Salli, I hope I'm not competing with Tom," I replied, a touch defensively. "But for so many years, I let him make the decisions about our shared world and our relationship. In New York, where I had my own friends and a career, it seemed to work okay. But once we left on this trip, I left behind most of the activities and people that grounded me."

I hesitated, wondering how much to explain. "By the time we reached Panama, I felt lost, adrift, disconnected. During our first year on the boat, I let Tom control our social life, let him make the decisions about the boat and our itinerary. It wasn't until Panama that I finally figured out how to stand up for myself. What you're seeing—I hope—is Tom and me learning to 'negotiate' when the things we want are different."

Salli stopped walking and faced me, her arms akimbo on her hips. "Hey, it if works for you, it's cool. But *you* asked me. My opinion is that you and Tom are in a constant struggle for control."

As I look back on that conversation, I would have been wise to explore her perspective, but I wasn't ready to deal with it yet. Changing the subject, I asked, "Have you decided what to send home to your family for Christmas?" For the rest of the walk, we talked about Tongan crafts—braided baskets, woven mats and tapa cloth wall hangings—along with recent additions to our shell collections.

When we got back to the dinghy, the tide had started to turn. Our shells were nowhere to be seen. "Salli, where'd they go?" I wailed.

She twirled in place, searching along the shoreline. "I can't believe somebody took them. We're the only ones anchored at Ofu."

"Maybe we left them farther down the beach?" I said, glancing both ways along the shoreline. "Let's walk a little and see."

She walked in one direction and I headed off in the other. About 30 seconds later, I heard her shriek. "Aha, the mystery is solved!"

"Did you find them?" I trotted over to where she stood, pointing to three of our shells.

"They've got hermit crabs in them." Grinning, she said, "Our shells just got up and walked away."

After half an hour, we'd managed to re-collect the shells, many of which had wandered as much as 50 yards down the reef. Neither of us hesitated to dispossess the hermit crabs.

Tonga offered much more than the Fearsome Foursome. It's the only Pacific island nation that's never been conquered by a foreign power and Tonga's king was determined to preserve the "Tongan Way." Many islands had no electricity or running water, and going ashore meant stepping back in time. The unpaved roads were used mostly by bicycles and scooters; what few cars and trucks were to be seen dated back to the 1950s. Commercial radio, TV and newspapers were almost nonexistent. In the stores, merchandise was stacked on shelves behind dark wooden counters, to be retrieved by a good-natured clerk when you got to the front of the line. Despite the heat, the Tongans wore clothes that covered most of their bodies.

Cruisers soon learned that the guys should not wear shorts or tank-tops when ashore. Women could wear pants and shirts, but if they wore a dress, it should be long sleeved with a high neck.

And yet, Tonga was up-to-date in some remarkable ways. Most of the farmers used modern agricultural techniques for fertilization and crop rotation. The king had also arranged for all fishermen to carry a handheld marine radio, so they'd never be at sea without access to help. Microwave relay stations towered above tiny villages where women swept pig shit off the dirt paths each morning.

It was a world much like we'd expected but failed to find in the Marquesas. Here, fresh food was abundant and cheap. The Tongans, fiercely proud of their traditions, needed little encouragement to tell you about them. Our introduction to the Tongan Way began one afternoon when a heavyset, elderly man, clad only in a t-shirt and dark blue, shin-length wraparound, rowed out to where we'd anchored in a bay near Neiafu. His smile stretched from ear to ear. As he pulled alongside, he handed me a large basket made from a banana leaf and filled with pineapples and mangos. His English was excellent, if a trifle formal.

"Welcome to Tonga. My name is Isaake. I hope you like mangos. I can bring you bananas or papaya if you would prefer."

Tom invited him aboard. I listened with fascination to Isaake's stories, each more colorful than the previous one. While Isaake made his living as a farmer, he told us he came from royal lineage, the second of several sons. Pointing to a wooden bungalow on the beach, a large and gracious if somewhat dilapidated clapboard house with floor-to-ceiling windows facing the water, he explained it had been built by a German missionary in the late 1800s. As the second son, much like in the English tradition, Isaake had inherited the house and a ceremonial role in the village, while his older brother served as a minister in the King's court.

As Isaake left, he invited us to dinner a few days later. I'd been struck by his generosity and wondered what I might offer him in return. Nothing that came to mind had the elegant simplicity of sweet ripe fruit in a handmade basket. With some hesitation, I offered him a bag of butterscotch candies for his grandchildren.

When we arrived for dinner, Isaake introduced us to his wife Anna, a slender, soft-spoken woman with a mass of thick, grey hair piled loosely on top of her head. After showing us around the house—devoid of furniture—he led us into the solarium we'd seen from *Salieri*. Intricately detailed handwoven pandanus mats covered the floor. A sofa and a small table, both white wicker, were the only furniture in the room.

He motioned for us to sit on the sofa while he sat cross-legged on a nearby mat. Anna brought in a large tray, laden with platters of fish, bread and vegetables. Laying it on the mat, she placed a section of banana leaf in front of Isaake and another in front of Tom. When she'd ladled several mounds of food onto the banana leaves, she sat on Isaake's left. Isaake began to eat with his fingers, motioning Tom to follow suit.

Anna and I watched in silence as the two men ate, also in silence. I had no idea when—or whether—Anna and I would eat. I couldn't believe they'd invite us to a meal and then not feed me, but I wasn't sure. Finally, when the men had finished a second helping, Anna filled another banana leaf and laid it in front of me. She filled one for herself. We, too, ate with our fingers, in silence, with the men watching.

Ill at ease watching the men eat and in turn being watched as I ate, I felt even more awkward trying to eat the soft shapeless foods with my fingers. Instinctively, I read the absence of silverware as primitive, the absence of furniture as poverty. The silence, as odd as it seemed, saved me from having to make conversation when I had no idea what to say. Even so, it struck me that Isaake was a very gracious host.

As things turned out, we saw Isaake each time we returned to Neiafu. Many aspects of his life felt familiar. A tireless worker, he ran a large and efficient farm on which he raised vanilla beans as well as fruits and vegetables, relying heavily on principles of crop rotation and modern techniques of fertilization. He doted on every member of his household, including several children and a dozen or so grandchildren. He was a deacon in the Methodist Church and encouraged us to come with him to church on Sundays.

Isaake admired many aspects of western culture, and I soon discovered he and Anna operated far more easily in our world than we did in theirs. When they joined us for dinner on *Salieri,* they sat on the settee, were adept with silverware and seemed unfazed by the four of us eating at the same time. Conversation flowed easily throughout the meal. As I got to know this thoughtful and generous man, I realized he was neither primitive nor unsophisticated. He was just different.

Out of respect, I wanted to be as functional in his world as he seemed in ours. I practiced sitting cross-legged until my knees bent easily, and I grew adept at eating with my fingers. Eventually, I came to understand that if you grow up sitting on the floor, chairs are uncomfortable, much as sitting cross-legged had been uncomfortable for me. If you grow up eating with your fingers, silverware feels like an affectation, a bit like chopsticks to a westerner. In a patriarchal culture, no one questions "why" the men eat first.

Perhaps the most profound learning experience came with my discovery that Isaake and Anna were wealthy. As a prosperous farmer, Isaake could afford to buy whatever he wanted... for Anna, a sewing machine powered by a small generator, for himself a motorbike. But they did not want much. Put another way, there were few things they valued that they did not already have...a comfortable house, plenty to eat, a large and healthy family. Furniture and silverware had no appeal for them. Appliances could break and had to be maintained. "We bought the wicker couch," Isaake eventually told us, "because so many yachties seem uncomfortable sitting on the floor."

Despite all the "stuff" we had on *Salieri*—books, music tapes, games, dishes, bicycles, tennis racquets—it struck me that we were poor by Isaake's standards. I began to reassess the value of the furniture, clothes and artwork Tom and I had so carefully stored in a New York warehouse, things that made life complicated, created worry and work. The simplicity of Isaake's life appealed to me. I wondered if my life would be simpler if the warehouse burned down.

One afternoon shortly before we were to leave Vava'u, Isaake arrived with a small wood and steel implement, crudely made. As he came aboard, he handed it to me. "A memento of Tonga," he said.

"Isaake, what is it?"

"A coconut scraper. I made it for you. Get me a coconut and I'll show you how it works."

Tom split a coconut with his machete. We watched with amazement when Isaake scraped out the hard, white meat as easily as if he were spooning out ice cream.

His gift, a response to a genuine need, had cost him nothing, but was priceless to us. I wanted to leave them a memento of our visit, something equally special. But what? I asked Isaake what Anna might like. Tom asked Anna what Isaake would like. Comparing notes, we found that both of them had responded with "nothing."

Having nothing to give them made me feel poor in a way I'd never felt before, even in my college days when I had no money. For days, I struggled to think of something I could leave with them.

"Would they like some books?" I asked one day over lunch, looking at the yards of bookshelves that surrounded us.

"No...the only thing they read is the Bible. Isaake says they already have about two dozen copies, gifts from yachties who preceded us."

Another time, Tom asked, "What about some cooking pots for Anna?"

"No," I replied. "Anna can afford to buy a pot if she needs one. Besides, I want to give them something of ours and we don't have any pots to spare."

And then one morning, as I made up the berth, I knew what my gift would be. Anna loved making clothes for her granddaughters. She could afford to buy fabric, but the selection of dark colors and fussy Victorian prints available in the Neiafu market did not appeal to her. Our sheets, while not new, had bright colorful designs and were wrinkle-free. I wrapped up one set of clean sheets and raced over to the house. By the next evening, her three granddaughters all had new dresses.

I felt richer than I'd ever felt before.

CHAPTER 14

PARADISE REVISITED

AS I sat in Father Phillip's study in the mountains of central Panama with a map of the Pacific Ocean, the island of Lifuka had seemed only a modest detour off the course from Vava'u to New Zealand. Only after arriving in Tonga did we learn that the Ha'apai, an archipelago straddling the tropical and temperate zones, had unpredictable weather, poorly charted waters and no protected anchorages. Cruising yachts were advised to give it a wide berth.

For Tom, sailing where other cruisers feared to go was just the sort of challenge he loved. Going there to deliver a package from a missionary we'd met in Panama made it all the more intriguing. Even so, we agonized over the decision for several weeks. Random coral outcroppings could damage our hull unless we maintained a constant vigil while under sail. Unprotected anchorages would leave us vulnerable to volatile weather, particularly if a sudden storm put us on a lee shore. But stormy skies would make it impossible to see the coral heads beneath the water, so leaving for another anchorage would not be an option.

We vacillated for several weeks, debating the pros and cons with everyone we met. When Salli and Dan offered to go with us, the die was cast.

The Ha'apai marked a watershed in our journey. Until then, Tom and I relied entirely on our own judgment about the risks posed by the wind, the currents and the seabed. We solicited others' ideas but made our own decisions. We offered advice based on our experience but took no responsibility for others' decisions. In the Ha'apai, the route we took, the places we anchored, how long we stayed, all would be shared decisions, a joint responsibility.

The expedition proved far less daunting than we'd feared. The sapphire blue water was crystal clear and the coral heads— stalagmites rising up from hundreds of feet below—were readily visible. The weather, ideal throughout our stay, made for comfortable anchorages. Because so few cruisers visited the Ha'apai, we were welcomed like royalty. The shared sense of responsibility created a powerful bond among the four of us.

We left Neiafu in the late afternoon and cruised through the night with starry skies and a beam wind. The northernmost edge of the Ha'apai appeared as dawn broke, and the sun stood high in the sky by the time we arrived in local waters. I positioned myself on the bow pulpit where Tom, at the wheel, could see my hand signals, much as we had done leaving Turks and Caicos. *Last Act* followed in our wake, with Salli on their bow and Dan at the wheel.

After an hour, I felt the strain of trying to read every small change in the surface of the water, and switched places with Tom. Salli remained on their bow. When Tom and I changed places after another hour, Dan called on the VHF.

"We're getting a bit of a free ride back here. How about if we take the lead for a while, so you guys can get a break?"

To my surprise, Tom agreed, and we dropped back behind

Last Act. Dan took the watch on their bow, while Salli steered. By the end of the next hour, we'd arrived in Lifuka.

We had the anchorage, located directly off the town center, to ourselves for our two-week stay. The four of us moved back and forth between the two boats as if they were rooms in one house. We ate most meals together. I napped on *Last Act* when the other three played cards or talked on *Salieri*. Salli often hung out on *Salieri* when Dan was deep in a boat project. Tom and Dan went on nighttime snorkeling or scuba expeditions in search of lobster. Salli and I walked the low-tide reefs, adding to the size of our shell collections and the depth of our friendship. We all slept long hours at night and for perhaps the first time in my life, I looked forward to an afternoon nap.

Our world went well beyond the space of the two boats. Through Chris, the Marist missionary to whom we delivered the package from Father Phillip, we entered into the life of the Ha'apai in a way we'd never anticipated. It began over dinner one evening, as Chris described his philosophy for educating island children who had no need to memorize the monarchs of England or the names of the continents. In Chris's eyes, his mission was to provide the islanders with the practical skills that would make their lives easier and safer.

"The problem," he said as he explained his rationale for the repetitive training that young boys got in repairing small engines and power tools, "is not a lack of mechanical aptitude. In fact, most of the boys can take apart an engine and put it back together again blindfolded. But only if they're asked to do it. If you don't ask, they won't do it."

Dan asked, a bit tongue-in-cheek. "Why not? Don't all boys love to take things apart?"

Chris sighed, having obviously given this explanation before. "Think about it, Dan. These folks have lived for centuries in a world where everything they eat, everything they wear, all their tools, come from the land or the sea. When something wears out—dishes made from coconut or clam shells, clothing made from tree bark, a canoe from a tree trunk—they simply throw it into the sea, where it disintegrates and returns to nature." He paused. "When it no longer serves its purpose, you throw it away. Their culture has no concept of maintenance or repair."

"Do they have the spare parts and tools to do the maintenance?" Dan asked again.

Chris nodded. "Yeah, they get that stuff when they buy the equipment. I'm talking about something much more basic—the notion of refilling the gas tank or changing the spark plugs or putting in a new drill bit when the old one gets dull. The training is to reprogram their brains so they remember to do it."

His curriculum included piloting, the art of finding a precise location on the sea from triangulating visible points on the horizon. Piloting would allow the boys to identify and return to fertile fishing grounds. Unfortunately, with Chris's limited budget, the students practiced compass readings with a plastic Boy Scout model that was only accurate within a few degrees. They could be half a mile from their target by the time they had gone a few miles offshore. They knew how to plot a course, but their charts, which covered almost the entire western half of the Pacific, proved useless for navigating around the Ha'apai.

The four of us, of course, had found Lifuka by piloting through the welter of islands. Both boats had precision compasses and detailed charts of the area. And so, we volunteered to run field trips. Each day for the next 10 days, except for Sunday, we took a group of eight teenaged boys, four on *Salieri* and four on *Last Act,* out to sea.

The boys arrived in school uniform, a shin-length, light-blue wraparound, a short sleeved white cotton shirt and bare feet. We made them plot the course, steer the boat and make corrections as they sailed in a predefined square two miles on each side. Energetic and curious, they took the exercises seriously and most groups could steer the exact course to the exact location by the second leg of the square. At the end of each trip, we made popcorn, something they knew of only from radio or television. The boys loved it, and each group arrived more eager than the one before!

Through Chris, we received an invitation to attend the dedication of a new Catholic Church on Ha'afeva, a nearby island. With the exception of Chris, we were the only foreigners at the three-day celebration presided over by the very regal bishop of Tonga. After consecrating a cinderblock church dedicated to St. Anthony, the bishop blessed the first communicants, ranging in age from 7 to 50, as well as the seemingly endless supply of fish and pork and taro and yams, all cooked in dirt pits covered with banana leaves and hot rocks.

With the holy work done, the bishop presided over the dancing from a throne-like chair on the church porch. Everyone else sat in a semicircle on the ground. The dancing began with a middle-aged man, the mayor of the island, wearing a long black skirt and an intricate but well-worn fringed tavolo, the woven ritual wrap that covers the hips and legs. Soon other men joined him. Next, three young girls in strapless sheaths of painted tapacloth came into the center of the circle. Their nubile bodies, shimmering with coconut oil, were a striking sight given the traditional modesty of the adults. As they danced around the circle, the congregation stuck pieces of paper money on their arms, legs and back. The girls scraped off the money, intended to support the church, as they danced on the porch in front of the bishop.

The Ha'apai, like Panama, proved both entertaining and educational. We left only because we had to reach New Zealand before the typhoon season set in. All four of us, teary-eyed as we raised the anchors and pulled out of the anchorage at Ha'afeva, knew that an amazing chapter had come to an end.

The Ha'apai reinforced our desire, first articulated in Panama, to experience life in other cultures. And so, as we made our way south toward New Zealand, Tom and I weighed the pros and cons of working in Auckland, a city of roughly a million people. We expected that our finance expertise would prove valuable, since New Zealand had only recently decontrolled its currency and interest rate markets. As itinerant travelers, our best option seemed to be consulting work. But the normal five-month "layover" during typhoon season hardly seemed long enough to find jobs and get integrated into the Kiwi way of life.

One sunny afternoon, Tom lounged in the cockpit with a calendar, counting off the months. "Let's assume we take six weeks to travel around New Zealand. We'll need at least two months to do the maintenance on *Salieri*. That leaves less than two months to work, even if we get jobs right away. I can't imagine anyone would hire us for so short a period."

"Well, if we stay more than five months, we've got to stay until the end of the next typhoon season." I counted the months off on the calendar. "That's roughly 18 months."

"It's our only option if we want to work." Tom grinned. "No guts, no glory."

A few days later, as I fixed yogurt and bananas for lunch, Tom came back to the subject. "It doesn't make sense for me to get a full-time job until the maintenance on *Salieri* is done. If I do the work on the boat, I can take my time to find the right job opportunity. Financially, it'll probably work out better than if I get a full-time job right away and we pay someone to do the maintenance."

"You've never liked being a nine-to-fiver anyway," I mused. "So, I'll look for a full-time job while you work on *Salieri* and explore the investment banking market at the same time."

Tom came to the galley counter where I stood slicing bananas and gave me a bear hug. "Mary, I think New Zealand is going to be a great place for us."

Little did we know.

PART IV

WEATHERING THE STORM

CHAPTER 15

SHOAL WATERS

IT was late October, the last night of our Pacific crossing. Eager for the sights, sounds and smells of civilization, we hugged the eastern shore of New Zealand as we approached Auckland, boundlessly curious about the world that went with the mapful of unpronounceable Maori place names—Waikaremoana, Whangarei, Kataia, Te Araroa, Whangaparaoa.

Our passage that night was a magical ride on a carpet of light. The starlit sky, banded by the Milky Way, was reflected on the water beneath our hull. Tom and I snuggled in the cockpit, watching the stars dance on the restless sea surface. Awed by the spectacle above and below, we were too excited to read or sleep. Mostly, we sat in silence, simply taking it all in.

The porpoises—perhaps a dozen of them—arrived about 4 a.m. I heard their squeals before I saw them. "Wow, they're here to take us in to Auckland."

As we watched from the foredeck, *Salieri* floated in a pool of luminescent foam where the dolphins broke the water's surface. Glittering strings of green-white light radiated from our hull in all directions—underwater strands of diamonds and emeralds.

"The dolphins must be setting off the plankton." Tom, his arm around my shoulder, leaned down and kissed my head.

I leaned into his hug. "With a welcome like this, Auckland has to be a wonderful place."

The porpoises stayed with us until just before dawn, when we passed the first of the residential communities on the north side of Waitemata Harbour. By noon, we'd cleared Customs and got *Salieri* tied up in our berth at Westhaven Marina, five minutes by car from the center of town.

We broke out champagne and stared at a chart of the entire Pacific Ocean—not yet believing we'd crossed 12,000 miles of water, 37 feet at a time.

The next two weeks went by in a blur, the passage of time marked only by the increasing brilliance of the "Kiwi Christmas tree." The majestic trees with their shiny dark-green leaves and the tongue-scrambling name of Pohutakawa line the boulevards of Auckland. Their lush red bottlebrush blossoms first emerge in early November and reach their peak in mid-December.

We devoted much of our time to household tasks. I spent days in the laundromat, using steaming hot water and mechanical power to wash out a year's worth of salt and mold. I luxuriated in the ability to put groceries in a cart rather than a string bag. Tom began maintenance on the winches, the navigational equipment and, of course, the diesel engine. We got our teeth cleaned by a real dentist and found a doctor who could relieve the rashes that had bedeviled us both since the Marquesas. We got professional haircuts.

But mostly we explored Auckland, one of the world's most beautiful cities. Once again we hauled out the fold-up bicycles that had given us so much pleasure since Charleston. Our daily rides took us, huffing and puffing, across the hills of Auckland. We window-shopped and went to the movies. We sampled ethnic restaurants, sometimes going out for both lunch and dinner. I joined the Tepid Baths (that really was its name!) and started lap swimming every morning. Tom joined the Royal Yacht Club and began to race in the Wednesday and Saturday regattas. We bought a 1971 Ford Cortina with a good engine but a decrepit body and christened it Rusty Bucket ("RB" to its friends). Many evenings, we partied to celebrate the arrival of another member of our Pacific cruising class.

I did miss Salli and Dan, who'd sailed directly to the Bay of Islands, at the north end of New Zealand, where they planned to spend the summer layover. When they came to spend a few days with us on *Salieri* in early November, life took on a delicious aura of timelessness and togetherness. Tom and Dan raced in the regattas. Salli and I scoured the boutiques in Parnell for local wonderments to send home for Christmas. We spent hours experimenting with local recipes for kiwifruit, tamarind and baby lamb. Dan and I compared books we read and pondered the pros and cons of returning to civilization. Tom and Salli provided an endless litany of ideas for adventures in New Zealand.

Life was good.

As has happened so many times in my life, I found a job because I was in the right place at the right time.

It began in Tonga during cocktails on an Alden ketch newly arrived from New Zealand, whose captain had spent a season working as an IT consultant. When we told him of our plans to work, he suggested we call the head of KPMG's consulting practice in Auckland. About a week after we arrived in Auckland, we invited Peter Ross to lunch.

To our dismay, Peter, an IT "nerd," showed no interest whatsoever in Tom's venture capital background or my commodities experience. Conversation lagged and I breathed a sigh of relief when lunch finally ended. Imagine my surprise, a few days later on a Thursday, to see Peter tromping down our dock, looking ridiculous in a suit, tie, brogans and a briefcase.

"KPMG," he said after he'd clambered on board, "has a client, a gold bullion dealer, who's found evidence of fraud. Unfortunately, no one in KPMG's New Zealand offices knows anything about running a bullion business, let alone how to deal with fraud." Peter offered me a job with a salary package that included a car. "Can you start on Monday?" he asked.

Peter's offer would disrupt our plans to tour New Zealand in early December. But as Tom and I talked over dinner that night, he agreed. "It's too good an opportunity to pass up." With a twinkle in his eye, he added, "And you'll make more than enough to support me in the style to which I'd like to be accustomed. I can work on *Salieri* and explore the investment banking market at the same time. It's perfect."

We broke out our second bottle of champagne and toasted our remarkable good fortune!

Ever the introvert, I was energized by the job in ways that sightseeing and parties could never do. It gave me endless stories about the perplexing people I met and the ridiculous *faux pas* I made as I tried to fit into a country that spoke a version of English that was all but a foreign language. As a fringe benefit of the job, KPMG made a number of introductions for Tom in the financial markets.

Tom and I fell back into the now-familiar pattern of parallel lives. But things didn't work quite as they had in the past. In New York, we'd talked by phone every afternoon. In Panama, where we both worked for Mel, our paths crossed throughout the day. In Auckland, without a phone on the boat, it was hard to keep in touch, to coordinate schedules, to make evening plans.

And then, one evening, early in my third week of work, I arrived home about 5:30 p.m. to find an empty boat. When Tom arrived half an hour later, laden with groceries and full of apologies for traffic delays, I forgot about it. But later that week, it happened again. No Tom. No note. No car. The night before, we'd talked about seeing a movie, so when he wasn't home by 7 p.m., I started to worry. I checked the bar at the Yacht Club. He wasn't there. I made the rounds of friends docked at Westhaven. No one had seen him since early afternoon. I checked the parking lot. His car was gone.

I grew more frantic as the minutes passed. I was on the verge of calling the police when he strolled in at 8 p.m. carrying his squash racquet and gym bag.

"Omigod, Tom, I'm so glad you're okay. I was afraid you'd been in an accident."

He looked surprised. "I played squash with Graeme at 5:30 and then we got a hamburger. I mentioned the game to you a couple days ago. I should have stopped by to tell you we decided to go out to eat. I'm sorry."

"Last night we talked about going to a movie."

Putting his arm around my shoulder, he gave me a hug. "There's plenty of time for a 9 p.m. movie. I'm so sorry if you've been worried."

His apology sounded so sincere, I couldn't stay mad. But when I replayed the scene later, I knew something was wrong. Perhaps he had told me about the squash game, perhaps I'd forgotten. But his original plans hadn't included dinner. It seemed appallingly inconsiderate to let me sit waiting. And he knew I didn't like late movies, even if I didn't have to go to work the next day.

A few nights later, when I arrived home, I found him asleep on the settee in the saloon with his breakfast and lunch dishes still piled in the sink. A bag of dirty laundry sat in the cockpit. Wondering if he was sick, I read for a bit and then started dinner. The noise in the galley woke him.

"Hi, sleepyhead. You okay?"

"Yes, I am. I am just tired," he said, surprisingly terse for someone who'd just woken up.

"How was your day? Anything exciting?"

"No," he shot back. "Nothing at all happened today. I spent all day right here, doing boat tasks. I didn't see anyone and I didn't go anywhere."

His self-pitying tone surprised me. "Tom, are you bored with being on the boat? If you'd rather be working and hire someone to do the maintenance, we can do that."

"Just leave it be," he grumbled.

His response made me uneasy. He was doing exactly what he'd said he wanted to do. And given how much encouragement he'd received during his job interviews, I was sure he'd be working within a matter of weeks.

My uneasiness mounted each time I came home to an empty boat. Invariably, Tom had an explanation. Once he pulled a note out of his pocket. "I forgot," he said looking abashed, "to leave it on the table." Another time, he returned from a late afternoon job interview. "I didn't know," he explained when he arrived back about 10:30 p.m., "that it included dinner."

His behavior seemed so out of character with the courteous man I'd married. And then, one afternoon as I tried to concentrate on a client report, I remembered how, in the early years of our marriage, he consistently walked a few paces ahead of me. During those years, I never seemed able to keep up, whether we were walking to work in the morning, hiking in the Berkshire Mountains in the afternoon or strolling home from the theater in the evening.

I tried to walk faster, matching my short stride to his longer one. No matter how hard I tried, though, I couldn't keep his pace. Other times, I asked him to walk more slowly. "I have to run to keep up with you," I complained.

When I asked, he would slow down. "I'm so sorry," he'd say. "I keep forgetting I walk faster than you."

But I had to ask, over and over and over again. Each time, it upset me a little more than the time before. Irrational as it seems, I was annoyed at myself because I couldn't match his pace. More reasonably, I was annoyed at his refusal to take account of my short legs. To top it off, I felt foolish for being annoyed at all, when he was so obviously willing to slow down if I asked. And then, one day, it dawned on me that he actually maintained the same pace I did, only a few steps ahead of me. The frustration often drove me to tears.

And then, one muggy Saturday evening in July, six years into our marriage, he walked into the dining room with two plates of strawberry rhubarb pie in his hands and a hangdog look on his face. I said, winking, "Tom, you look as if you'd been caught with your hand in the cookie jar!"

Putting the plates down, he spoke slowly, almost as if the words stuck to his tongue. "There's something I need to tell you...but I don't want to."

I grinned, presuming he'd forgotten to do something or said something foolish, and patted his hand as he sat down. "Well, with an intro like that, you have to tell me, don't you?"

When he didn't grin back, I had a sense of foreboding.

Staring at his plate, he spoke in a voice barely above a whisper. "Mary, for years you've complained about my walking ahead of you. I did it on purpose."

"You're kidding...why?"

I could barely hear his response. "As stupid as it sounds, I always wanted to marry someone tall and blond. Marrying you felt like failure. Walking ahead of you allowed me to hold on to my fantasy."

I sat bolt back in my chair. "You knew my height and hair

color long before you married me," I blurted out. "Why *did* you marry me?"

He sounded sheepish. "I felt so childish. I kept hoping that loving you would make it go away."

My words tumbled out before I could edit them. "So you punished me for your immaturity. Did I get that right?"

He continued to stare at his plate, saying nothing.

"That's the most ridiculous thing I ever heard," I spit out. "I didn't want to marry someone bald but, Jesus, I got over it in the first month."

Still, he didn't say anything. As I waited for his response, outrage replaced my initial disgust. I wanted to slap him. Instead, I got up and took the dishes out to the kitchen.

Only when I began to scrape plates into the garbage disposal did the import of his words—that I'd shared my life and my bed with a man who was embarrassed by me—sink in. With no warning, I threw up everything I'd eaten all day.

For the next few weeks, I fought the urge to vomit every time Tom touched me. Gradually, though, I came to realize the courage it had taken him to speak up after so many years. As the weeks passed, I noticed that he walked by my side without my having to ask.

Now, 10 years later, he seemed to be punishing me once again. I had no idea why.

Things came to a head one night in mid-December, about six weeks after I started working. For several hours, I sat waiting, with no idea where he was. The whirling mixture of anger and anxiety made it impossible to read. When he finally arrived about 9 p.m., I protested. "Tom, this has happened too many times to believe you forgot to leave a note. What's really going on?"

"Goddammit, Mary, I spent 24 hours a day with you for nearly a year. Wasn't that enough?" He glowered at me. "I don't want to spend every goddamn minute of my day with you now. Can't you give me some space?"

His comment made no sense, since I spent all day at work. Why was he complaining about spending every minute with me? And then the emotion behind his words hit me. My knees went weak and I sat down to avoid falling. *Tom doesn't want to be with me.* I flashed back to those lovely months in the Western Pacific, aghast at the thought that he might have been pretending.

I tried to keep my voice calm. "Tom, I'm not asking you to spend all day with me, I'm only asking you to let me know when you'll be home so I won't worry, so I'll know if I should make my own plans."

Tom's retort was chilling. "Mary, you don't need to worry about me. You do whatever you want, whenever you want." He pulled a book off the shelf and sat on the settee. Without another word, he started to read.

Tears spilled down my cheeks. Something in our relationship had snapped. And I still didn't know why.

Much as we had in Charleston, we carried on with the motions of daily life even as our emotional relationship grew increasingly strained. The boat got cleaned, the laundry got done, the bills got paid. We made friends through my job, through the marina, and through his contacts in the financial markets. We enjoyed a steady stream of movies, dinners and parties. Our active social calendar gave us plenty of reasons to avoid dealing with our growing estrangement.

Increasingly, we traveled around the North Island by car, exploring the wine country, the 90-Mile Beach and historic Maori villages. For Thanksgiving and again for Dan's birthday in late January, we drove to the Bay of Islands. Starting in January, we began house-sitting for Auckland friends on extended trips overseas. Over the next nine months, we lived four houses, each quite distinctive. All offered us more space but not necessarily more comfort than on *Salieri*. I enjoyed having a big kitchen and Kiwi cookbooks, but longed for the warmth of the boat when I got out of the shower in an unheated house in the middle of winter.

With so many friends who had boats, we went sailing regularly. Waitemata Harbour, with its myriad volcanic islands, offered an almost infinite choice of scenic anchorages, whether we wanted a day sail, a weekend away or a vacation. Less than 30 miles from downtown Auckland, it was easy to find a deserted cove with pippies (sand oysters) and mussels in abundance. We did most of our cruising on *Salieri*, but while her fiberglass hull was being repaired, we sailed with Kiwi acquaintances or Dan and Salli, who came to Westhaven, once in mid-January for engine repairs and then again in late February to get *Last Act* ready for the passage back to San Francisco.

I was most content when Dan and Salli came to Auckland, in part because Tom became more affectionate and engaged when they were around. He was acting out a charade, but in fairness, I played it, too. While I had come to think of Salli as one of my closest friends, I never said a word to her about my increasingly hollow marriage. I didn't know what to say.

Salli and Dan's departure for the U.S. at the end of April left a large hole in my life. Although I liked my job, it often frustrated me, occasionally on issues of principle, more often on issues of style or form. When Tom and I found ourselves alone, conversation seldom extended beyond routine household matters. We never talked about our relationship or about the next phase of our cruise. We never made love. Tom no longer kept me guessing as to his whereabouts, but he spent as little time alone with me as he could decently manage.

Each time I asked why he'd become so remote, his response was a variation on the same theme. "Mary, there's nothing wrong with our relationship. Stop worrying so much" or "You're being paranoid. Of course, I love you" or "It's unrealistic to expect the emotional intensity we had in the Pacific. But that doesn't mean I don't love you."

He always sounded sincere, but I didn't believe him.

In July, when we'd been in Auckland for eight months, our house-sitting took us to an elegant affair in the upscale neighborhood of Remuera. Tom had been busy with consulting projects and a few days after we moved in, he flew to the States for two weeks. About the same time, I started on a new consulting project, work that suited me well with people I enjoyed.

During his absence, I spent much of my free time reading or writing about the passage across the Pacific. I spent hours in the glass-enclosed breakfast nook, ensconced in a white wicker rocking chair, bathed in sunlight, the scent of jasmine wafting in from the garden. Gazing out over the patio, my eyes feasted on arbors overflowing with crimson bougainvillea. Surveying the kitchen, I found a brilliant white space adorned with primitive blue and yellow pottery.

In that magical spot, life no longer seemed so grim, and by the time Tom returned, I was more upbeat than I'd been since our first weeks in New Zealand. My renewed optimism and good humor would, I was sure, vanquish whatever barriers had grown between us.

It was not to be. Tom returned even more remote and uncommunicative than he'd been before he left. A few days after his return, I broached the subject over dinner.

"Tom, I'd wish you'd tell me what's wrong."

His tone impatient, he replied, "Why do you keep harping on something being wrong?"

My voice had a pleading tone, despite my effort to sound conversational. "Tom, you never spend any time with me unless you have to. We don't make love and you turn away when I reach out for you. I know there's something wrong."

His response was curt. "Mary, I'm so tired of your imagining problems where they don't exist. I love you. I've told you that a hundred times. I don't know how to make it any clearer."

I didn't believe him. But then, a few days later, he strode into the kitchen where I was fixing dinner. As he put his attaché case down on the dark-green granite counter, he said, with a joviality I hadn't heard in months, "You better show some respect here, kiddo, you're now talking to a Vice President of NZI."

I hadn't expected that. As far back as Tonga, he'd insisted he didn't want a nine-to-five job.

"Congratulations," I said brightly. "So...tell me. What made you decide to take the job?"

"I can do so much more with the resources of NZI than I can on my own. And..."

I interrupted, "...but you've known that since the interviews began three weeks ago."

He gave me an impish grin. "...they offered a lot more money than I expected. I know how much you'd like to travel in Asia. I'll make enough for us to go anyplace you'd like, and go in style."

My heart started to pound...for the first time in months, he was thinking about me, about us. Then my skepticism kicked in. "Tom, you spend too much time at work to take a job you don't want. Traveling isn't important enough for you to spend your days in a bureaucratic environment you don't enjoy."

"It isn't just the money. Really, it's not," he insisted. "NZI has several challenging projects they want my help on."

Putting his arm around my shoulder, something he hadn't done in months, he reached into his case and pulled out a bright yellow envelope. He gave me the envelope, along with another big grin. "How'd you like to spend Christmas in Thailand?"

"Wowww. I'd love it." I felt lightheaded, almost giddy. Could the months of misery have been simply because Tom resented my having a steady job when he didn't? Would his working at a well-paid, high-status job allow us to reclaim our marriage?

With every fiber of my being, I hoped so.

CHAPTER 16

PARADISE LOST

AS the rising plane banked steeply over the volcanic hills, above the gray-green gum trees bent from years of the ferocious Wellington winds, I shivered. Why? I wasn't cold. Perhaps a tremor of pleasure? *What a nice week!*

As we reached cruising altitude, my mind wandered to the consulting job at Rural Bank, an analytical project I could handle easily while greatly expanding my knowledge of the financial markets. My peers, all very capable, possessed a range of extracurricular interests that promised some entertaining lunch and dinner conversations. My apartment on The Terrace, a renovated garret with a panoramic view of the city, was too good to be true. It was a perfect base for Tom and me to explore the South Island over the next three months.

I shivered again. Suddenly, I knew why. I was nervous about seeing Tom...more than nervous. I was afraid. Things had improved since those first months in Auckland, when Tom had been so intent on rejecting the intimacy of our days in the Western Pacific. Once he joined NZI, the day-to-day surface of our life—bicycling, sailing and dinner with friends—became undeniably pleasant.

But still we never talked about personal things, about what we wanted out of the Auckland experience, about the rest of the voyage, or about life in general. Our conversations about even day-to-day events often felt scripted, devoid of energy or spontaneity. Tom was never openly rude, but neither was he affectionate. We hadn't made love in months. Too often, I felt I was invisible to him.

As he'd become more distant, I'd grown increasingly reluctant to offer a gesture of affection or share with him what I wanted or how I felt. Day by day, I'd been shaving off bits of my personality to avoid anything that might spark a negative response, a gesture of rejection. For most of the summer, I'd felt alone, helpless and a bit numb.

Now, after a week in Wellington, I felt alive and energetic, eager to say and do what came spontaneously. The thought of facing Tom's indifference yet again brought a lump to my throat. Swallowing hard, I turned in my seat, staring out over the New Zealand coastline and the Tasman Sea so my seatmate wouldn't see my tears.

"Helloooooo...I'm home," I called out cheerily as I came through the front door.

"...in the kitchen," I heard Tom reply.

He stood at the counter, slicing pâté. Clad in plaid shorts, a green polo shirt and tassel loafers without socks, he looked so preppy, the boyish fellow I'd met on a ski slope so many years before. I didn't even mind that his once thick mop of curls had receded to a wispy fringe around a shiny pate. For the millionth time, I was turned on by his well-muscled calves and high ass. I put my arms around his waist and planted a kiss between his shoulders.

"Hi, Mary-pie. I missed you." He gave me a one-arm hug, his knife still poised over the pâté. The words sounded right, but his tone was flat, without affect. The gesture was right but his hug, over before I could lean into it or hug him back, had no warmth. I swallowed hard and told myself I was overreacting.

"I missed you too, kiddo," I heard myself say. In fact, I'd hardly thought about him until I got on the plane. I wondered if my voice sounded as flat to him as his had to me. After less than three minutes at home, I'd started to analyze every word, every gesture, once again incapable of taking anything either of us said or did at face value.

"Hummh. How was Wellington?" Tom asked, his attention already back to slicing pâté.

My mind was racing. I barely heard his question. I needed to think, to get myself back on an even keel. "Let me change my clothes. I'll tell you about it while I help you fix dinner."

"Great," Tom responded, his voice still flat. I forced a smile as I left the kitchen, but it hardly mattered, since he didn't look up.

I changed into shorts and a cotton shirt and sat on the edge of the bed, soaking up the last of the golden afternoon light. Breathing deeply, I tried to calm my mind. *I'm so tired of feeling everything I say or do is wrong.* I had the horrific image of finding my mother in the kitchen when I went back.

But with that image came the realization—a shocking one—that I was doing to Tom exactly what I blamed him for doing to me…mouthing words I didn't mean and affecting emotions I didn't feel. *Is Tom's remoteness my fault after all?* And yet, after the week in Wellington, it didn't feel like my fault.

When I found the courage to go back to the kitchen, Tom had hors d'oeuvres ready on the porch, and was decanting a New Zealand merlot. As we watched the sunset, he talked about his latest deal at NZI. The project, an unusual mix of finance theory and politics, genuinely interested me. But his voice had little inflection and he never paused long enough for me to comment or ask questions. Throughout, he looked into his glass of wine or out over the hills, just starting to turn green in the September spring. He never looked at me or caught my eye. It was a lecture, not a conversation. Absorbed once again in analyzing his stiff body language, his flat tone of voice, I took in little of what he said about the project.

When we'd finished the first glass of wine, we moved to the dinner table. Tom brought me up to date on re-rigging *Salieri*. Again, his eyes rested everywhere but on me. I felt a lump in my throat, hurt that the details of a sailboat were more compelling to him than my new job.

As his words washed over me, I wondered why he didn't ask about my week. And then, with a jolt, I realized he *had* asked—in the kitchen when I first got home. But I'd walked away from the conversation. *It is my fault.*

I took a deep breath and began to describe the job and the people, emphasizing humorous things that had happened during the week. But still, he didn't look at me. He wasn't listening. I found myself talking faster and faster, lecturing him as he'd lectured me on the porch. I stopped in mid-sentence, frozen with a fear I could not name.

"Tom, what's going on? We're talking at each other, going through the motions of conversation. It feels like you wish I wasn't here." Once again, my mind was running on a separate track. *Mary, you're accusing him of not wanting you, when the truth is that you don't want to be here.*

"Of course I'm glad you're here. I missed you this week." He was looking out the dining room window.

"But, you haven't smiled at me once."

Now staring into his wine glass, his response sounded weary. "Mary, you're so paranoid. Why does everything have to be about you?"

"I don't know what else to think when you won't even look at me."

He did look at me then, a direct and unyielding gaze. "I've had a tiring week and I'm having trouble concentrating on much of anything."

"Did something happen?" I asked.

"No, I'll be fine after a good night's sleep." He stared into his wine glass again. "Look, let's get a video. That's about all I'm up for tonight."

Leaving the dishes undone, we went to the video store, settling on *The Hustler*. Although I'm a big Paul Newman fan, I couldn't concentrate. *Maybe he did have a tough week. Maybe I am paranoid.* My breathing grew erratic, short gasps that didn't let enough air into my lungs.

As the film wound on, I flashed back to Remuera, the over-sized wicker chair in the bright white kitchen with the scent of jasmine, the memory of the contentment I'd felt in those weeks. I wondered why I hadn't been able to hold on to that feeling of calm.

A few minutes later, I found myself thinking about Nassau, two years earlier, when *Salieri* had been tucked into that tiny and ever-so-friendly marina. That too had been a lovely time, my days filled by interviews with other midlife cruisers and a string of interesting lunch and dinner conversations. Again, I wondered what had caused the mood to break.

And then, towards the end of the film, I remembered. Each of those times, Tom had been away and I'd been on my own, much as I'd been in Wellington. Like tonight, he'd been aloof when we came back together, giving me no sense that he was happy to see me. Like tonight, I'd tried to share my delight but cowed by the blank look on his face, I'd eventually given up.

I can't do this again. Desperate to put some space between myself and Tom, I forced myself to stay put until the movie ended and he got up to rewind the video. As calmly as I could muster, I said, "I'm going back to Wellington tomorrow morning."

Without looking up, he asked, "Are you that busy after only a week?"

I tried to keep my voice steady. "No. Something's been wrong between us for months. Every time I try to talk about it, you tell me I'm imagining it. But it's not my imagination. I want some time on my own to try and figure it out."

Tom, the VCR cassette in his hand, finally looked up, a perplexed look on his face. "This is so unlike you," he said.

As tears began to roll down my cheeks, he went on. "Mary, can we talk about it in the morning. I'm too tired right now."

I'd heard that line before. It didn't work this time. "No," I said, "I'm going back on the first plane."

A pleading expression suddenly appeared on his face. "I don't want you to leave me. I couldn't bear losing you." He didn't move from the VCR player, but the intensity in his voice surprised me. I hadn't said anything about leaving him.

"I'm not leaving you, Tom. I just want a little time on my own."

For the next hour, Tom talked without cease, insisting that he loved me. He talked about our shared adventures and our shared values, about the opportunity to spend time together in Thailand at Christmas. I listened, wanting desperately to hear words of love. But as hard as I listened, I couldn't hear love or feel tenderness in his voice. He never asked for any explanation of why I felt the way I did.

Throughout his speech, he remained at the opposite end of the small couch. He never took my hand or patted my shoulder. When I reached out to stroke his arm, he pulled away. The pain of his gesture stopped my breathing completely.

When I could breathe again, I stood up. "I'm going to bed."

As I walked toward the door, he said, "We'll talk next weekend when I come to Wellington."

To my own surprise, I turned and looked him directly in the eye. "I don't want you to come next weekend." I walked out.

Ten minutes later, he appeared in the bedroom doorway, a grin on his face, the same idiotic grin he'd had before he told me about wanting to marry a tall rich blond. Leaning his shoulder against the doorframe, he crossed his arms on his chest, his body stiff. "There's something you ought to know." He paused. "I'm in love with Salli."

I stared at him. "Sally who?"

"Salli Paxton."

Assuming it was a sick joke, I said sarcastically, "Salli and Dan left for the States in May, four months ago."

"It started last February when she and Dan brought *Last Act* to Auckland for the engine repairs. It began as just a fling, but at some point we fell in love."

My mind went blank. Swallowing hard to avoid throwing up, I finally managed to respond. "Soooo...there really has been something wrong all these months. Why did you insist that it was all my imagination...that I was paranoid?"

Tom unfolded his arms and held them out in front of him, a gesture of explanation. "I still love you." He hesitated, "I'm glad this is out in the open. I need your help. I don't know what to do."

My laugh was thin. "Tom, you must think me a perfect fool. Right this moment, I don't give a damn what you do."

By the time I crawled into the bed in the guest room, I had no laughter left in me, but I couldn't cry either. I was shocked that I'd never suspected, still more shocked that my friend Salli—the tall blond of Tom's fantasy but also the woman who taught me to trust—had betrayed me as well.

Sleep would not come. I struggled to understand. Had their affair started because of our failing marriage or Tom's still-lingering adolescent fantasy? Was he angry at me for having a job when he didn't? Did Salli initiate it or Tom? And Dan...did he know? Why had Salli been ripe for this affair? What had I missed in the months we traveled together?

For a brief moment, I grew cynical, wondering if Tom had made it up to punish me yet again.

Unable to sleep, I hugged my pillow and tried to stop my mind from racing. At first light, I left for the airport without waking Tom and wondering how I was going to make it through the day.

CHAPTER 17

ADRIFT

THREE weeks went by before I saw Tom again. It would be wrong to say I was happy during those weeks. I felt fragile and burst into tears at unexpected moments. But once over the initial shock, I felt a curious sense of relief. Looking back at our 10 months in Auckland, I knew Salli wasn't the problem. For whatever reason, our marriage had effectively come to an end only a few weeks after I went to work, many months before their affair began.

Then, too, I had plenty to distract me. The consulting job was challenging and time-consuming. I found Wellington to be a cosmopolitan city and had amiable companions for the movies, theater, symphonies, jazz clubs and dinners. And then, halfway through the first week of October, Tom called.

"Mary, I'd like to come to Wellington Friday afternoon."

Still unsure whether I wanted to fight for my marriage or just walk away, my response was not welcoming. "What for?"

His breathing sounded uneven. "Mary, I've done some pretty stupid things. I'm so sorry. I love you more than I can say. But I'm confused. I need to talk to you." He sounded on the verge of tears.

Listening to him, I wanted to cry. I still loved him. I wanted him to love me. Reluctantly, I said, "Okay, but come Saturday. I have plans Friday night."

"I don't mind being alone Friday evening for a while if you're going out."

Determined to protect the space I had finally created for myself, I forced my voice to sound hard. "I don't want you to come Friday. Come Saturday morning."

I barely recognized the man who arrived Saturday. Never, even in our courtship days, had he been so willing to explore his feelings about me or our relationship. Never had I seen him so determined to understand his own motivations or the patterns in his life. Never had he expressed such interest in how I felt.

Even so, it was a painful weekend. I wept as he explained that what I had viewed, over the years, as mouthing hollow responses had not been an attempt to fob me off. "Mary, I tried to say the right words, hoping the right feelings would somehow follow. But I never seemed to get it right."

I was dismayed as he described his recurrent sense of impotence as he stood in the hall of our apartment listening to my sobbing in the shower. I felt guilty as he described his frustration with my mood swings and my pathological fear of being ignored or discounted, his inability to anticipate how I'd react to anything he said or did, the burden he carried in trying to satisfy my need for constant reassurance.

As I replayed those conversations, I realized how badly I'd misinterpreted his aloofness. True to my mother's training, I read his blank looks as rejection. It had never occurred to me they might reflect his uncertainty, his need for me to reach out to him. No doubt about it, I thought, this is really my fault.

...and yet, the longer I listened, the more I knew it wasn't all my fault. He'd belittled my enthusiasm and energy when he might have asked me to share it. He'd denied his doubts and insecurities when he might have asked me to understand them. He'd accused me of paranoia when he was unwilling to acknowledge his own frustration or anxiety. Perhaps my childhood baggage had caused me to over-react, but I hadn't made it all up.

And then, of course, there was Salli. We didn't talk about her much, but her image hovered in the background. When I asked, he admitted that "leaving you and going to her is an option." Grimacing, he continued, "I've come to Wellington because I have to decide."

In between soulful conversations, we strolled up and down the hills of Wellington. After a candlelight dinner Saturday night overlooking the Bay, we made love with considerable passion. Each minute felt real, sincere, honest. Even so, I was relieved when he left Sunday evening.

Over the next few days, I made up lists—why we should stay together, why we should call it quits. When I looked at how open and thoughtful he'd been over the weekend, I felt hopeful. But when I examined the destructive behavior patterns we'd developed over the years, I grew skeptical. I vacillated hourly about our chances—indeed, about the desirability—of staying together.

His visit left me sad, much sadder than I'd been before his visit, now vividly aware that something in which I'd invested so many years might be gone, that I could lose the emotional ballast that came from Tom's everyday good humor, from his morning smile. But curiously, I wasn't depressed. Losing Tom didn't feel like losing control. Indeed, I felt more in control of my own life than I ever had before.

Given my history of depression, that was a big deal.

Ten days after his visit, early on a Wednesday, Tom called from the Auckland airport. "I'm waiting for Salli's plane. She's coming for a week. I have to see her again before I decide whether to try to fix our marriage or whether to just bag it."

All the air suddenly got sucked out of my lungs. "Why are you telling me this?"

He hesitated. "I want to be honest with you."

I hung up, a flash of white light bursting behind my eyes. *That damned son-of-a bitch. He wants to have his cake and eat it too.* During our weekend of "honest" communication, he hadn't said a thing about having Salli come to visit. Why, I wondered, does he have to tell me this now, when he kept her a secret for six months?

By the time I got home from work that night, images of the two of them filled my mind. I cried myself to sleep and awoke Thursday morning immobilized by the thought of what they might be doing. The thought of their sharing a laugh devastated me nearly as much as the thought of their sharing my bed.

At work, I couldn't focus on conversations, couldn't make even minor decisions, couldn't remember what I should be doing from one minute to the next. On Friday, I left for a long-scheduled weekend in Marlboro Sound on the South Island. For hours, I drove aimlessly through the yellow gorse-covered mountains, seeing nothing, trying desperately to calm my mind. I felt utterly alone. No one in the entire world knew where I was. At one point, maneuvering through a series of hairpin turns on a narrow dirt road, a road high enough that I could see the Sound across the hills, I wondered how many times my car would roll if I decided to go straight ahead at the next turn.

I didn't go straight. But the thought that I might have driven off a mountain road scared me, big time. When I got back to my hotel, I called Kay, the one person I knew in Auckland, but she wasn't home. In desperation, I called Tom. In my confused state, I forgot Salli was there and sobbed helplessly when she answered the phone. When she handed the phone to Tom, I tried to tell him, choking over my tears, how frightened I was.

"Darling, please don't do anything to harm yourself. I love you so much." His words stopped my sobs. Had I heard that right? He hadn't called me darling since we arrived in New Zealand.

In the next breath, Tom said, "Mary, I'll stay on the phone as long you want. Don't worry." We sat on the phone, mostly in silence, for about 20 minutes. Finally, I began to calm down. As I hung up, he said, "We'll be home all evening. Call back whenever you want."

Despite a cold, drizzly rain, I went for a walk along the beach. My panic had passed and I started thinking about Salli. Only a few weeks earlier, I'd viewed her as a friend. Now, trudging along the beach, I realized I still did. I wanted to know why she'd been ripe for an affair. I wanted to see her. Somehow, I knew she'd come if I asked.

Bizarre as it might seem, I called her when I got back to the hotel and asked her to visit me in Wellington. She arrived midmorning two days later and stayed until the last flight out.

We talked without cease, sometimes stretched out on the floor in my garret, sometimes walking along the quay. She described a marriage that seemed the polar opposite of mine. Dan, she explained, "idolizes me. He wants to know everything I think about, everything I feel, what I ate for lunch, how I spent my morning. He has me on a pedestal."

As I listened, I thought how much I would love to have a man who genuinely cared what I said or did, a man who wanted to take care of me. I had no idea what that felt like.

And then, to my astonishment, she announced, "It's an intolerable burden. He expects me to be perfect—to look perfect, to do everything 'just so.' I never quite live up to his expectations. For years, I've felt suffocated, as if I might suddenly be unable to breathe."

I did know how she felt.

She surprised me again when she said, "But I don't think it can work with Tom. We're too much alike." She paused. "I need someone who's a good listener, someone who likes being protective. I don't think Tom's capable of being that person."

"So, why did you come to Auckland?"

She hesitated. "I didn't know until this week. Last summer started out as a fling, so it didn't matter what kind of a person he was." Shaking her head, she grimaced. "...fact is, I still love Dan."

She paused, blinking back tears. "But, Mary, I've really screwed up. When I left for the airport, Dan said he'd change the locks if I wasn't back in three hours. He'd do that. I'm not sure I'll have a place to live when I get back."

Salli's visit grounded me. In a comic moment, we'd talked of throwing over both guys and traveling together ... of writing a soap opera called "Love in the Laundromat"...of setting up a *ménage a quatre*. We laughed until our sides hurt. In honor of our many shopping expeditions, we bought a host of totally frivolous things to eat for dinner.

I gathered strength from her unexpected weakness. Her ambivalence made me realize that she would not make a serious claim on Tom. If I wanted to make my marriage work, the opportunity was still there.

Tom called in late October, his voice strong and convincing. "Mary, I love you and I want us to stay together."

I wondered if that's what he really wanted. Or did he just not want to be alone now that Salli had walked away from their affair?

I wanted to believe he wanted me. And so, on November 3rd, I moved into Tom's house on John Street. I remembered moving into our first apartment on Central Park West so many years earlier. *Am I doing this because I want to be with Tom— or just so Tom will love me?*

Chapter 18

Charting a New Course

AS I rounded the corner onto John Street, I saw Tom's car parked in the driveway. My breathing went shallow. The two weeks since my return to Auckland had been a rollercoaster ride. Tom vacillated daily between loving me and hating me, between a conviction that our marriage had to be saved and an equal certainty that he wanted out. He didn't talk about Salli, but I knew Dan had locked her out and filed for divorce while she was in Auckland. I was never quite sure, as I drove home from work each night, whether he'd still be there.

In truth, I was never quite sure whether I wanted him to be there. His intermittent but obvious efforts to open the lines of communication gave me hope that we could recapture and build on the companionable intimacy we'd had in Tonga and the passion that had burst forth that weekend in Wellington.

Even so, my desire to stay with Tom diminished with each passing day. Still as vulnerable as ever to that blank expression on his face, invariably moved to tears when he avoided my efforts to show affection, I found myself longing for the freedom of movement I'd had in Wellington.

The Sunday after I got back, we went sailing for the day. As we steered *Salieri* out of the marina at Whangaparoa, Tom was affectionate, patting me on the butt or giving my shoulder a kiss as he went by. But as the hours passed, I noticed that if I took the initiative, he looked back at me blankly. Once, when I leaned over and hugged him, he stiffened. When I tried to seduce him during our lunch stop, he said he'd eaten too much. For perhaps the millionth time, I felt silly, school-girlish, immature for wanting my husband's attention.

But that day, for the first time, some part of me realized that wanting my husband's affection was perfectly appropriate...that it was his blank look and passive response that were unreasonable.

Suddenly, I remembered Salli's comment in Tonga about Tom and me struggling for control. Flashing back to our Wednesday and Saturday lovemaking schedule in New York, it struck me for the first time that Tom needed to be in control of the giving and taking of affection. With that thought, I felt a huge weight being lifted off my shoulders.

Waiting to fall asleep that night, my mind wandered back to times when I'd been alone—Nassau, Remuera, and the first week in Wellington. As I lay in the dark, puzzling over the way my good humor had dissipated each time Tom and I'd come back together, a pattern emerged. Each time, Tom had belittled or ignored the energy and enthusiasm I'd found when he wasn't with me. As I listened to Tom's steady breathing, I rearranged the pieces of the puzzle. One piece fell into place. *That's it. Tom doesn't like it when I'm happy without him.*

Another piece. *It's not his fault that I couldn't maintain my own sense of delight unless he shared it. It's not his fault I was so insecure. And why didn't I try to jolly him along, cajole him into sharing my highs? Why did I give up so easily?*

I sat bolt upright in bed as yet another piece fell into place.

Or maybe, if I'd been more self-confident, I would have left him years ago, while the highs and lows were still part of my daily life.

I knew, as I lay back down, that much of what had gone wrong had indeed been my fault. But for the first time, I understood that my mistake had been unconsciously ceding to him the right to judge what I should do and how I should feel. I needed to take more responsibility for my actions and feelings. But I also knew that changing my behavior would be pointless if Tom persisted in being aloof and uninvolved. Unless he too could make some changes, our marriage would end.

I realized I couldn't wait much longer. I finally fell asleep.

A few days after that middle-of-the-night insight, as we drove home from dinner with friends, Tom reached over, patted my knee and then moved his hand lightly up and down my thigh. Once home, his moves were slow, gentle, loving. Afterwards, I fell asleep in his arms, and dreamt we were walking on a beach in Tonga at sunrise.

At breakfast the next morning, Tom looked up from the morning paper and said in a matter-of-fact voice, "Mary, I've decided. I'm leaving."

I put my coffee cup down with a thunk and stared at him. "You're kidding. What was last night about?" My voice sounded shrill. I paused, trying to get my bearings. More calmly, I said, "Tom, you were reaching out to me in a way you've never done before."

He laid his right hand over mine. "Mary, I love you more than you'll ever know. But there are too many scars, too much baggage. I can't do this any longer."

Minutes passed, neither of us saying anything, our eyes searching each other, his hand still on mine. I struggled to balance his words with the feeling of his body in mine the night before. His words echoed what I'd been thinking with ever-increasing clarity, but the timing puzzled me. Had the emotional intensity of our lovemaking scared him?

Amid tears flowing uncontrollably, I had an unexpected sense of relief. Tom had made the decision I hadn't had the courage to make. Drawing my hand out from under his, I got up from the table and called Kay who agreed to meet me for lunch. As I hung up the phone, I heard Tom leave the house.

Over lunch, Kay consoled me as I wavered between relief that the indecision was over and grief at the loss of a 16-year habit. She listened patiently as I dithered about whether to go home to New York or continue traveling by myself – staying in Auckland simply was not an option I considered. She offered me their guest room for as long as I wanted.

"Why did you wait for him to make the decision?"

Unable to answer her question, I babbled on about loving him despite his flaws, about the importance of his laughter in my day, about his obvious efforts to work on our relationship. With each reason, I reiterated my determination that now, finally, it was over.

When I got home after lunch, I started to pack. About 4:30 p.m., when Tom returned, he called up the stairs, his tone somber, "Mary, come sit with me in the garden for a bit. I'd like to talk."

My response was tart. "I'm packing. I want to be out of here by dinner time."

"Please."

My response was sharper than I meant to sound. "There's nothing to talk about."

As I continued to sort through drawers, I heard him trudge up the stairs, his footsteps slow and heavy. My lungs got tighter, my breathing shallower with each step. When he came into the bedroom, a room too small to have a comfortable chair, he settled on the floor against the wall where he could catch my eye.

With tears streaming down his face, he blurted out, "Mary, I made a terrible mistake this morning. Last night scared me. I love you so much. I don't want to leave you."

I took a long breath, trying to force air into my lungs. Fighting annoyance, fatigue and frustration, I said brusquely, "Tom, you don't know what you want. I can't do this any longer."

Looking up at me with swollen eyes, he pleaded. "How do I make you believe me?"

The sarcasm in my voice reflected my scorn. "Your changes of heart don't exactly strengthen your case."

"Mary, I want us to be together."

"Have you told Salli that?"

"No, but I'll call her right now."

"Why didn't you tell her before you came upstairs? Are you still hedging your bets?"

Still looking up at me, Tom shook his head slowly. "Mary, maybe I'm doing this all wrong. I don't have a lot of practice. But I really want things for us to work."

I put down the clothes in my arms and looked directly at him. "Tom, you had it right this morning. The scars are too deep. The bad habits are too ingrained. We both need to move on. If you want Salli, fine. If you don't, fine. But you and I are history."

He stared at me for a moment and then picked himself up off the floor and went downstairs. For ten minutes, I listened to his sobs as he paced back and forth on the bare maple floor. I could feel my resolve wavering. Wondering if I was making a terrible mistake, I went downstairs.

He looked at me with sad eyes as I stood on the landing. "Mary, I've hurt you and I'm so sorry."

For reasons I will never fully understand, I walked over and put my arms around his neck. "Tom, I'll give it one more try. But I won't live with the specter of Salli any longer. She's got to be out of your life, completely."

Tom's relief was almost tangible. "I'll call her now."

I went back upstairs, debating whether or not to undo the packing I'd just finished. While I couldn't hear the conversation, I heard him go into the garden after only a few minutes. Wondering if a short conversation was a positive omen, I looked out to see him slumped on the wooden bench under the kumquat tree. He didn't look happy. I decided not to unpack.

About 15 minutes later, I heard him coming up the stairs two at a time. Slouching against the doorframe of the bedroom, Tom's familiar grin lighting up his face, he said, "Well, kiddo, it's you and me from here on out."

Incredible as it seems, I felt a burst of love. Tom had chosen me. In Tonga, we'd come so close to the relationship I'd always dreamed of. This time, I thought to myself, it will really last.

Now, as I saw his car in the John Street driveway, I knew it wouldn't last. Tom had become increasingly withdrawn, making it ever more obvious that he was tortured by second thoughts. He paraded his distress in what I saw as a self-indulgent and childish way, expecting me to be sympathetic and understanding about what he had given up, yet offering me no words of affection or reassurance in return. Each time he turned away from me when I reached out to him, my anxiety ratcheted up another notch. As I approached the house that evening, I sat heavily in the driver's seat, exhausted by the effort of trying to understand his needs even as I knew that I had to protect myself.

Turning into the driveway, I saw Tom peering out the front window. He waved. I wondered what he'd been looking for. When I came through the front door, he gave me a bear hug and handed me a glass of chilled white wine, at the same time running his fingers around my neck and down my back.

"I thought about you a lot today," he said with a sly smile. I took the bait. "And what exactly did you think about?" He gazed steadily at me. "That I love you so very much." His fingers moved softly up and down the ridge of my spine.

"Aren't we supposed to leave for Kay's birthday party pretty soon?" I asked, playing the flirt.

"Yeah…but no one will notice if we're a little late. I can think of something I'd rather do right now."

"Hummh," I said taking the bait again, "why don't you tell me what it is?"

"I'd rather show you" he said, taking my hand and leading up the stairs. He undressed me, slowly and romantically, but once foreplay began, his moves became increasingly mechanical. His erection partially subsided. Within moments, I knew his mind was elsewhere. I waited for it to be over. When he was done, he got up wordlessly and went into the bathroom.

I wondered, as I listened to the shower, if this was how a hooker felt. More than any other time in our marriage, I felt I'd been used, a nameless vehicle for satisfying Tom's urge.

Tom's casual manner when he came out of the bathroom struck an odd note. I nearly jumped two feet when he patted my butt as I walked past him to take my shower. It got odder. As we dressed, he maintained a steady patter, talking about his day, asking about mine. The pleasant banter felt out of place after a week of silence and, just now, an impersonal sexual transaction.

And then, as we were walking out the door, Tom said without looking at me, "Don't you think it's a positive sign that our sex life is becoming spontaneous?" I nearly choked. It hadn't been spontaneous. He'd been waiting when I got home. He'd planned this. Something was wrong.

We knew a lot of people at Kay's party and for a while I was absorbed in conversation. And then, on my way to refill my wine glass, Kay stopped me in the hall. "What's with Tom?" she asked. "He's not his usual jovial self."

"I don't know," I replied, suddenly aware that Tom and I had not been in the same conversational group even once. In the two hours since we arrived, he'd never looked at me or caught my eye. I remembered that night in September when he wouldn't look at me, the night I decided that Wellington on my own was better than Auckland with Tom

"How are you two doing?" Kay continued.

"A week ago, I thought we could make it work. But with every passing day, I'm more skeptical."

"Well, Mary, I hope it works out the way that is best for both of you, whatever that is."

During the drive home after the party, Tom looked despondent, his responses to my questions about the party unenlightening—"Brad didn't say much," "the conversation with Susan wasn't very interesting."

I tried another tack. "Tom, you seem down. Is something the matter?"

"No. Just tired."

I'd heard that line before. Riding the rest of the way home in silence, I felt the knot in my stomach wind tighter with every passing block.

Unable to stand the tension, I blurted out as I hung up my coat, "Tom, what in hell's going on? This isn't about being tired."

He started up the stairs, not looking at me. "Mary, I'm exhausted. I want to go to bed."

I felt a rush of adrenaline. "That's bullshit. Tom, you made love to me tonight as if you were a robot. And you haven't looked me in the eye all evening."

He stopped on the landing, without responding. He was looking at his feet.

I went on, "A week ago, you said you were committed to us, but it feels like you've already left."

As I said the words, I knew what had happened. I walked over to the landing and pushed his arm, swiveling his body to make him face me. "You've talked to Salli, haven't you?"

"Don't ask unless you really want the answer," he replied, his glare hard and unyielding.

"I already know the answer," I shot back, certain that he had called her. "But why?"

"Because I love her."

My stomach hurt like hell. I pushed him again, until his back was up against the wall. "So...why that ridiculous seduction routine tonight?"

"I was horny for you," he said, his eyes back on his feet. "I still do love you."

"Horny for me or horny for Salli?" I could hardly get the words out. As the reality of his action sank in, I was horrified. "You were using me, weren't you?"

He wouldn't look at me. I jabbed his arm several times. "Answer me, Goddammit."

Finally, he responded, a whispered response I could hardly hear. "No."

I was shaking with anger, an inch from slapping him. Through all of our ups and downs, I'd always viewed Tom as honorable. He'd often avoided the hard places in our relationship, but I'd never seen him as intentionally cruel or willfully deceiving.

For weeks, I had vacillated, torn between the need to break away from a marriage that wasn't working and the desire to save a marriage that had brought me personal growth. But now, finally, I was ready for the step I had to take.

My words came out slow and steely. "Tom, we're done. You'll need to find a place to sleep tonight, because you sure as hell aren't sleeping here."

After he left, I paced the house for an hour or so, dry-eyed, reliving the conversations and conflicts of the past two months. As I paced, I remembered my reaction to his first decision a week earlier…a blend of surprise, disappointment and relief. This time, I was devastated. His deceit made even the good parts of our marriage seem fraudulent and demeaning.

I paced until exhaustion overcame me, well after 3 a.m. Too tired and distraught to even get undressed, I simply fell onto the bed. Within moments, the tears flooded out. Sometimes hugging my pillow, sometimes kicking my heels against the bed, I sobbed until I finally fell asleep, just before dawn.

When I woke late the next morning, it was warm and the light was very bright but softer and easier on the eye than one expects from the glare of the noon-day sun. I could hear music, a lyrical and happy melody I didn't recognize. My heart swelled with exuberance. I wanted to dance.

And then I really woke up. It was only 9 a.m., a cloudy day. The music had vanished. Remembering last night's conversation with Tom, I started to cry again.

Every day for weeks, that dream came to me. Day by day, in those brief moments of magic, the lens with which I looked at the breakup of my marriage shifted imperceptibly. As the days passed, I began to see my marriage through the eye of my soul rather than the logic of my brain. The message was clear: while the collapse of my marriage stripped me of familiar and comfortable routines, it also released me from shackles I had not known I wore.

For so many years, I felt enriched by the laughter Tom brought into my life, but I never allowed myself to calculate the cost of his persistent lack of interest in how I felt or why. His gregariousness opened so many doors for me, but his disinterest in my emotional life closed down so many conversations that might have brought us closer. The boundaries of my outer world expanded because of his sense of adventure, but my inner world, my spirit, atrophied in the face of his disdain for my enthusiasm and energy.

The message of the dream was that the fretful, anxious young girl willing to pay any price to draw laughter, social pleasantries or adventure into her life, had been replaced by a woman who could make her own laughter, find her own friends, concoct her own adventures.

No doubt I had Tom to thank for many of these skills. But I no longer needed him to get through a day. Indeed, the message of Nassau, of Panama, of Remuera, and now of Wellington, was that I might well enjoy the day more if Tom was not a part of it.

A few days after New Year's, I got up, moving automatically through my morning routine—a shower, hot coffee and the morning paper. As I pulled out of the driveway en route to work, I sensed something missing. I had forgotten something.

It bugged me until, sitting at a stoplight a few blocks later, I realized that the dream was gone. For the first time since our separation, I had set about my day without the dream and without thinking about Tom. No delight at the lyrical melody, no tears at what I'd lost.

By the time the dream vanished for good, I had set myself on a new course. Having given up my New York career to see the world, I planned to see a lot more of it before I went back home. I booked tickets to travel through Asia and the Middle East for five months, some of the time backpacking on my own, some with an adventure-oriented tour group. With my itinerary in hand, I resigned my job in Auckland and accepted one in Melbourne, Australia, to start when my journey was done.

As I plotted out the next chapter of my life, I often thought back to those moonlit nights in the Western Pacific. As *Salieri* headed down the dancing moonbeam, I wondered what magical adventures I might find at the end of it. Having discovered how to be content with the moment, I was curious, but in no hurry to find out.

Although the end of that moonbeam remained far in the distance, I was determined to follow it. Though it would no longer physically mark my course as each day passed, it would continue to fill me with the power of potential and the joy of the journey.

Salieri's Itinerary 1985 – 1987

Arrival Date	Departure Date	Location	Days on Shore	Days at Sea
1985				
	8-Sep	Larchmont, NY		
8-Sep	25-Sep	Intra Coastal Waterway	17	
17-Sep	18-Sep	Annapolis, MD	1	
21-Sep	25-Sep	Norfolk, VA to Albemarle Sound	4	
25-Sep	26-Sep	Alligator River, NC	1	
25-Sep	3-Oct	Belhaven, NC	8	
3-Oct	10-Oct	Intra Coastal Waterway	7	
10-Oct	23-Nov	Charleston, SC	44	
23-Nov	25-Nov	at sea		2
25-Nov	27-Nov	Cape Canaveral, FL	2	
27-Nov	2-Dec	Stuart, FL	5	
10-Dec	18-Dec	Duck Key, FL	8	
18-Dec	27-Feb	Marathon, FL	71	
1986				
27-Feb	28-Feb	at sea		1
28-Feb	2-Mar	Bahamas - Chubb Cay	2	
2-Mar	27-Mar	Bahamas - Nassau	25	
27-Mar	17-Apr	Bahamas - various islands	21	
17-Apr	30-Apr	Bahamas - Georgetown	13	
30-Apr	9-May	Bahamas - various islands	9	
9-May	11-May	at sea		3
11-May	18-May	Turks & Caicos	7	
18-May	20-May	at sea		2
20-May	23-June	Dominican Republic	33	
23-Jun	2-Jul	at sea		9
2-Jul	18-Jul	Panama - Colon	16	

Arrival Date	Departure Date	Location	Days on Shore	Days at Sea
18-Jul	31-Jul	Panama - San Blas	13	
31-Jul	29-Jan	Panama - Pedro Miguel	182	
1987				
29-Jan	5-Feb	at sea		7
5-Feb	20-Feb	Galapagos Islands	15	
20-Feb	21-Mar	at sea		29
21-Mar	24-Apr	The Marquesas Islands	34	
24-Apr	2-May	The Tuamotus	8	
2-May	6-May	at sea		4
6-May	21-Jun	Society Islands - Tahiti	46	
21-Jun	27-Jun	Society Islands - Moorea	6	
27-Jun	10-Jul	Society Islands - Huahine	13	
10-Jul	18-Jul	Society Islands - Bora Bora	8	
10-Jul	28-Jul	at sea		18
28-Jul	9-Aug	Nuie	12	
9-Aug	12-Aug	at sea		3
12-Aug	22-Sep	Tonga - Vava'u	41	
23-Sep	13-Oct	Tonga - Ha'apai	20	
13-Oct	24-Oct	at sea		11
24-Oct		Auckland, New Zealand	____	_-_
			692	89
		miles traveled = 13, 612		